AF541262

# INTELLIGENCE AND PERSONALITY OF PROSPECTIVE TEACHERS

# INTELLIGENCE AND PERSONALITY OF PROSPECTIVE TEACHERS

*By*

**Mr. Gittaboina Sreenivas**
*M.Sc., M.Ed., M.Phil.*
*Bharat Heavy Electricals Limited*
*Hyderabad, (Andhra Pradesh)*

***Editor***

**Dr. Digumarti Bhaskara Rao**
*M.Sc., M.A., M.A., M.Ed., Ph.D.*
*Principal & Research Director*
*R.V.R. College of Education*
*D-43 (277) S.V.N. Colony*
*Guntur – 522 006*
*(India)*
*digumartibhaskararao@rediffmail.com*

**DISCOVERY PUBLISHING HOUSE PVT. LTD.**
**NEW DELHI-110 002**

*Published by:*
**Tilak Wasan**

**DISCOVERY PUBLISHING HOUSE PVT. LTD.**
4383/4A, Ansari Road, Darya Ganj
New Delhi-110 002 (India)
*Phone* : +91-11-23279245, 43596064-65
*Fax* : +91-11-23253475
*E-mail* : parul.wasan@gmail.com
discoverypublishinghouse@gmail.com
*web* : www.discoverypublishinggroup.com

***First Edition:* 2012**

**ISBN: 978-93-5056-101-0**

**Intelligence and Personality of Prospective Teachers**



***Printed at:***
***Shree Balaji Art Press***
***Delhi***

*Dedicated*
*to*

**Mr. K. Srinivasulu**
*M.A.(Lit.), M.Ed., P.G.C.T.E., M.Phil. (Edn.)*
*Assistant Prohibition and Excise Superintendent*
*Guntur-522002*
*Andhra Pradesh*

# Preface

Intelligence is the ability of adjusting in a new situation. It is the property of recombining our behaviour pattern so as to act better in a novel situation. It is the ability to adjust oneself to a new situation.

Personality is a stable system of complex characteristics by which the life pattern of the individual may be identified. An individual is characterized and distinguished from others by his personality.

The prospective teachers are the teachers in making. They need good personality and high intelligence to meet the cognitive and affective need of students after becoming the teachers in secondary schools. Hence, this study on the intelligence and personality of prospective teacher has been undertaken for a study.

The prospective teachers studying in Colleges of Education are with a bright average level of intelligence and with a highly extrovert personality. Except gender, the locality, the methodology and the qualification of prospective teachers show an influence on the level of intelligence and personality of prospective teachers.

The prospective teachers, the teacher educators and the social and educational environment should make the prospective teachers feel comfortable during their course period. The prospective teachers should enhance their intelligence and personality by better strategies. Better skills, good relations with peers and teachers, good teaching learning material, audio-visual aids, good instruction, self motivation, academic achievement, adjustment, yoga and meditation, better study habits, good life skills, appropriate aspirations etc. will help the prospective teachers in enhancing their intelligence and personality. The prospective teachers should develop and improve all of the above in order to master the teacher education skills, knowledge and to become expert teachers in future after rolling out of the Colleges of Education.

**Dr. Digumarti Bhaskara Rao**
digumartibhaskararao@rediffmail.com
Tele-Mobile: +91 949 3333 555

# Contents

# Chapter 1
# Introduction

"Genius is one per cent and ninety-nine per cent perspiration."

*—Thomas Alva Edison*

Children and youth vary in intelligence, personality, aptitude, interests and achievements. However, schools tend to emphasize the importance of differences in intelligence and personality.

## INTELLIGENCE

In contrast to animals man is considered to be endowed with certain cognitive abilities, which make him a rational being. He can reason, discriminate, understand, adjust and face a new situation. Definitely he is superior to animals in all such aspects of behaviour. But human beings themselves are not all alike. There are wide individual differences. A teacher easily discovers these differences among his pupils. Some learn with a good speed while others remain lingering too long. There are some who need only one demonstration for handling the tools properly while for others even the repeated individual guidance brings no fruitful result. What is that causes one individual to be more effective in his response to a particular situation than other. No doubt, interest, attitude, desired knowledge and skill etc. count towards his achievement. But still there is something that contributes significantly towards these varying differences. In Psychology it is termed 'Intelligence'. In ancient India our great Rishis named it 'Viveka'.

In educational world the term 'Personality' has a wide significance. Education is considered with an all round development of the personality of a child, therefore, it is quite essential for a pupil teacher to know about the term personality. Personality includes the totality of one's behaviour and hence both inner and outer (covert as well as overt) behaviour should be taken into consideration. In dealing with various aspects of the situations in our life, especially the ones connected with teaching and learning, one is bound to encounter the peculiar style in which each teacher behaves and each learner receives instruction. The behaviour of a teacher implies lot of social skill or adroitness and an influence direction arising from the salient impression which one creates on the other. In all this, there is manifest a distinct or unique method of approaching or influencing one another. This uniqueness of a person is generally known as 'personality'.

There are many other contexts in which we come across the phenomenon of personality. In the family, the personality of the housewife, in the club the personality of its members, in the school, the personality of the Principal or Headmaster, in the office, the personality of the chief executive and in the Government the personality of its leader determines the nature of interactions and the ethos of the organization to a considerable extent.

Intelligence is a native capacity and not an acquired one. It is manifested in different mental activities. It is the ability to learn to make use of acquired knowledge in new and complex situations. It is the ability to think abstractly, to solve problems, to perceive relationship and to profit from experience.

## Types of Intelligence

The four types of intelligence are the concrete, abstract, social and emotional intelligence. The ability of an individual to comprehend actual or concrete situations and to react to them adequately is concrete intelligence. Abstract intelligence means the ability to respond towards numbers and letter, etc. Social intelligence means the ability of an individual to deal with social situations. Emotional intelligence is the capacity to reason with emotions in four areas namely: (i) awareness – to perceive emotion; (ii) acceptance – to integrate it in thought; (iii) attitude – to understand it; and (iv) action – to manage it. An emotionally intelligent person controls all his emotions and sees that unfavourable incidences are not repeated again and again. The key domains of emotional intelligence are: knowing one's emotions, self-awareness, managing emotions, motivating one's self, recognizing emotions of others-empathy and handling relationships.

## Intelligence Tests

In the ancient period, measurement of intelligence was on the basis of knowledge or learning. In ancient literature the dialogue between Indra and Brahaspati and in Mahabharata between Yudhishthir and Yaksh is an olden form of intelligence testing. In the mediaeval age, intelligence testing was on the basis of physical structure. In 18th century Gall and Spurzheim tried to measure the intelligence of the individuals on the basis of the measurements of the skull. In the modern era, testing of intelligence is by accepting it as a natural and innate power. In 1905 Binet in association with Simon, undertook the task of devising test which could help the detention of mentally deficient children. This scale consists of 30 tests. They are arranged in an order of difficulty. In 1908 Binet started finding out mental age of the children. The idea of mental age was utilized in 1908 Revision of the Binet-Simon scale. When the Binet-Simon scale of 1908 was used on children and its results reported, some of the weaknesses of the tests were brought to light. In order to remove these anomalies, the scale was revised in 1911. The Stanford-Binet test of 1916 was standardized on a sample of 1000 children of whom 905 were between five and fourteen years of age. It includes 90 test items. In 1937 Terman and Merrill Revision or Second Stanford-Binet Revision test was standardized on 3000 children in eleven states of U.S.A. In 1939, David Wechsler has contributed a scale along with Bellevue and called it Wechsler-Bellevue theory which was meant for adults. In 1955 the Wechsler Scale was revised and they called it Wechsler Adult Intelligence Scale. The first scale of intelligence prepared in India by C.M.Rice of Lahore in the year 1922 and he called it Hindustani-Binet Performance Scale.

The general belief is that children learn faster and better than adults. Studies on learning and age relationships indicate that the ability to learn new material increases until the age of 16 years. Therefore, it remains constant till 20's after that there is a slight drop. Apart from these differences, we find a number of differences in the way people conduct themselves in various situations of life. People differ in many traits of personality. Personality traits appear to be products of a totality of interacting organismic and environmental influences.

## Uses of Intelligence Tests

1. Used for the purpose of making selection of the suitable candidates for activities like admission in a particular course of instruction, deciding the cases of scholarships, choosing candidates for participation in various co-curricular activities etc.
2. Help the teacher to classify the students as bright, dull or average and bringing efficiency in teaching learning process.
3. Promoting the individuals not only in educational fields

but in all other occupational and social situations where one studies to go higher on the ladder.

4. Revealing the potentialities of an individual and predicting one's success in a particular field to give guidance, helping in learning process and to establish a proper level of aspiration.
5. Exceptional children like gifted, backward and the mentally retarded children can be detected with the help of intelligence tests and helps in the diagnosis of the root causes of problematic behaviour of the child and like-wise suggest the possible remedy.
6. Useful in Psychological, Sociological and Educational research. For example in deciding the relative role of heredity and environment in the process of growth and development, research workers have made much use of intelligence testing.
7. Reveal the mental age or mental level of a child. It indicates the educability or readiness of a child for learning.
8. Indicates the need for providing teaching materials at different levels of difficulty.
9. Help the teachers in having homogeneous grouping among children.

## Abuses of Intelligence Tests

1. Intelligence tests cannot accurately estimate the intelligence of the individual.
2. They may develop complexes like inferiority and superiority.
3. The teachers form only permanent ideas on the students.
4. They may show partiality.
5. Classifying them into different groups may bring differences in the students.

6. Intelligence of the individual is dependent on other factors like health, mood, time of the examination, etc.
7. Intelligence is innate and fixed.
8. The intellectual development reaches a peak in adolescence and then gradually declines.
9. Calculation of IQ requires the chronological age of the child. But sometimes parents hide the real age of the child. Thus IQ becomes unreliable.
10. For children who are handicapped in the use of language, verbal intelligence tests cannot be applied.
11. Unless experienced and trained persons are available the scoring and interpretation becomes invalid.
12. Intelligence tests especially individual tests are too costly. Thus, ordinary teachers cannot purchase and make use of it.
13. IQ tests assess abilities that are too narrow and tell nothing about creativity, motivation, honesty, friendliness, and other human traits and characteristics.

## PERSONALITY

Ordinarily, Personality is taken as the external appearance of the individual. In philosophy the meaning of personality has been interpreted in the sense of the internal self. But in psychology neither is the personality the external appearance nor is it the internal self, but it includes both and much more. The word personality has been derived from the Latin word 'persona'. The word persona was used for the cover, utilized by the actors to change their appearance, but in the Roman times it was taken as the particular character itself. This second meaning has been taken in the modern word personality. Thus personality is not a fixed state but a dynamic totality which is continuously changing due to interaction with the environment. Personality is known by the conduct, behaviour, activities, movements and everything else concerning the individual. It is the way of responding to the environment. The way in which an individual adjusts with the external environment is personality.

Behaviour requires integration. This integration of various traits is found differently in different persons. As a general rule every healthy individual has some sort of integration. The peculiar forms of integration in a particular individual are his personality traits. Thus, personality is the most characteristic integration of an individual. It is personality which marks distinction in one man and another.

The personality is the integration of internal and external activities. It includes the external appearance, qualities, aptitude and capacities, etc. It is the result of the inter-action of the individual with the environment. It is not a collection of the traits, but a particular organization of them. It is the total quality of the individual's behaviour. Individual affects other individuals through his personality. Thus, personality is manifested in his various activities. In short, personality is the total quality of the behaviour, attitudes, interests, capacities, aptitudes and behaviour patterns, which are manifested in his relation with the environment.

The compulsive personality is characterized by excessive cleanliness, orderliness, obstinacy and stinginess. In extreme cases, behaviour becomes repetitive and ritualistic. Psychoanalysts believed that this personality structure arose through excessive cleanliness training in the period of early infancy.

The authoritarian personality is said to arise out of extreme parental rejection or domination in childhood, leading to repressed hostility. Such a personality structure includes highly conventional behaviour, superstition, destructiveness and cynicism, desire for power and concern over sex.

The Upanishadic thinkers looked upon Atman, the self as the basic concept equal to the concept of Brahman, the universal.

## Indian Personality

According to Gita, the man who is a tattvavit, who knows the truth, realizes that he does nothing at all and all are reflexes and bodily reactions. The higher self is one's friend and the lower self is one's enemy. The lower self consists of reflexes, bodily needs, feelings and emotions and the higher self manifests itself when the individual has gained full awareness of his needs and limitations. According to Nyaya, personality consists of the self, the atman, the manas, mind and the body. Gautama states that the self is a unique substance to which all cognitions, feelings, and actions belong as its qualities. The self controls and synthesizes activities of the mind and the body. It is the self that is responsible for the unity of all the various cognitions and actions. Man's behaviour and personality are governed by the defects which arise out of the delusion. So the remedy is to overcome false knowledge and acquire true knowledge. Thus the mental apparatus consists of the subtle body, but it cannot function without the physical body. The subtle body contains the samskaras, the impressions from the past experience. Every experience leaves an impression behind and becomes a samskara. Every cognition takes the form of the modification of buddhi.

## Aspects of Personality

The three aspects of personality are the dynamic aspect, the economic aspect and the topographic aspect. The dynamic aspect of Freud consists of id, ego and super ego. Id is the raw self of the individual which has no contact with reality. It is based on pleasure principle. It has unconscious instinctive impulses, frustrated desires and repressed feelings which very much influence the conscious life of an individual. Ego is the self of the individual and it is in contact with reality. It has the concept of time, distance and reality. It controls the animal wishes of the id and in turn is controlled by super ego. So the ego has control over the id. Super ego is called conscience to the ordinary sense. It is also known as Ego ideal. It is a counter check over the id and keeps the ego under control. It allows the individual to follow moral, ethical and social values.

The economic aspect consists of Eros and Thanatos. 99.5 per cent people have the instinct to live i.e., eros, to think to live, to be happy, to do good to self and others, to do constructive work to self and society and improvements in any area. Normally eros is present in all and it is natural. Thanatos is the death instinct. It is the instinct to die, to do destructive work to self and others verbally or physically. Now-a-days in normal persons also thanatos is dominating since many are committing suicide and passing on physical comments. So let Eros be dominated.

The topographic aspect of personality consists of consciousness, pre-consciousness and unconsciousness. It is the arrangement of physical structure in some aspect. The conscious state is a state of awareness and tells what a person does at present. Pre conscious state is a layer just below the conscious state in which the recent incidents are stored. The material from the preconscious level can be brought to conscious level with little effort. The deeply lying layer of the mind is the unconscious state in which are stored our childhood experiences, wishes and desires. The matter from unconscious level cannot be brought to the conscious level. But, Freud said that with a special technique, hypnosis, some of the unconscious experiences can be brought to the conscious level. According to Freud, by observing (conscious behaviour) only 1/8th part of the personality can be assessed. Remaining 7/8th part is subconscious and unconscious behavioural personality. The part which we cannot see is unconscious.

A number of techniques can be used for personality testing — interview, observation, self-ratings and personality inventories, check lists, rating scales, situational or behavioural tests, projective techniques, anecdotal records, autobiography and the daily diary etc.

## Types of Personality

Gita describes three different typologies based on the three gunas, the typology based on mortality and the typology based on social classification. Human nature is composed of the three elements called gunas or qualities, namely sattva, rajas and tamas. The three gunas are mingled in varying quantities which bring about differences in qualities. But the self is above and beyond these three qualities. Tamas the principle of inertia is passive and suffers all shocks. It is driven by the kinetic power of rajas which is embraced by an innate though impossesed preserving principle of harmony and balance and knowledge, the sattva. The man dominated by tamas develops a personality which is prone to confusion and delusion. This type is characterized by inattention, lack of understanding, indolence and languor. The person in whom rajas is predominant is given to attachment to the objects of desire. He is full of unrest, lustful and greedy. He is a creative of impulses and emotions. The man dominated by sattva guna is characterized by intelligence and clarity of vision. His desires and emotions are under control. He is free from lust anger and greed. His actions in society are motivated by the well being of the whole society.

According to Charaka 3rd century BC, human beings are divided into three classes on the basis of three gunas. The Brahman type of man is pure, devoted to truth, self controlled, with good memory and understanding, free from desire, anger, greed, conceit, envy and equally well disposed to all. The Rishi type is one who is devoted to study, yagnas, celibacy. The third type is Indra who is endowed with lordship and is authoritative in speech, who is brave and energetic.

There are six varieties of rajas type which are Asura – valiant, Rakshasa – cruel, Pisacha – bullies, Sarpa – rouses fear, Preta – covetous and Sakuna – fickle and intolerant. The three groups in the tamas type are the Animal type – un-intellectual, fish type – greedy of food and plant type – lazy and devoid of mental ability.

The Ayurvedic thinker Sushruta, 3rd century, classified people according to the preponderance of the three doshas — Vata, Pitta and Kapha. The Vataja is wakeful and dishonest, Pittaja is bold, eats a lot, irritable and cools down quickly, has good memory and intelligence. The Kaphaja temperament is grateful, self controlled and unselfish.

## Uses of Personality Testing

- Helps the students in proper educational and vocational choice.
- Helps the individual in resolving emotional conflicts.
- Helps the teacher and counselor.
- Helps the clinical psychologist to choose the best therapy for his patients.
- The teacher can understand the cause behind the deviant behaviour of the child to some extent.
- The teacher may educate the parents about effective child-rearing practices and healthy relationship between parents and their children.
- The teacher can ensure that the atmosphere in the school inter-personal relationships between the teacher and the child, teacher's expectations and behaviour patterns, quality of teaching, etc. are all conducive to the well being of the child.
- The teacher, in collaboration with his colleagues, should adopt good healthy practices in the school.
- The teacher can refer the child to appropriate professional personnel for treatment, if the child is found not curable in the regular school programmes.

### Difficulties in the Measurement of Personality

- Personality is not the thing; it is an abstract idea which is not clear to measure. It is a dynamic process which is ever in a process of change and modification from time to time.
- We do not find satisfactory instruments which are exact, reliable and valid for measuring the personality.
- In assessing the personality we are not interested in a person's best behaviour but want to find out his typical behaviour in ordinary situations.
- A person who is being questioned about his personality may not be reluctant to disclose information that will show him in an unfavourable light.
- Besides, obtaining an accurate picture of a person's personality the psychologist often has to ask questions about sensitive areas, such as the person's emotional adjustment to life, his relations with other people, his intimate family history and his attitudes. This can be constructed as an unwarranted intrusion in the privacy of an individual.
- The subject's reluctance to disclose sensitive information.

## ENHANCEMENT OF INTELLIGENCE AND PERSONALITY

- To promote greater educational attention to individual needs of pupils and to make best use of attractive abilities, their interests and expertise in teacher's community.
- To make the classroom teaching effective according to the interests and capacities of the pupil.
- To encourage flexibility in grouping the pupils. In this, the grouping of the pupils in a subject is done according to the interests and aptitudes of the pupils.

- To increase the quality of the instruction.
- To develop community sense.
- To conserve and promote the Indian culture and civilization.
- To involve the individuals in the social welfare.
- To evaluate whether the pupils are really deriving greater educational value from the 'enriched' and 'vitalized' programme than they do formally.
- To re-establish faculty 'esprit de corps' and school morale to assess in various ways the degree of improvement in personal and professional attitudes in human relations.
- To estimate the success with which guidance procedures, differentiated programmes of study, courses and units of learning experience, individualized teaching and learning procedures and other educational measures designed to achieve greater satisfaction of individual needs.
- To realize the fact that the so called general intelligence tests are not actually general but it measures some specific abilities.
- To achieve desirable goals by meaningfully involving teachers in making and carrying out plans that effect intelligence and personality, providing an atmosphere of acceptance, support and understanding, and helping people experience feelings of worth, helping people make sound judgements and act on the basis of careful study of adequate and accurate information.
- Do everything possible to improve student's physical condition. Various studies have shown that improvements in health may lead to marked gains in IQ scores as well as in capacity for steady intellectual growth.

- Make certain that students have maximum opportunity for achieving new and higher quality perception. Perception occurs only when a meaning is grasped.
- The capacity of a person to improve his perceptions may be increased of some of his most pressing goals are met.
- We can help the student to achieve more useful perceptions if we try to hand perception to him independently which helps in fostering intelligence and personality.
- Schools should do what they can to help children achieve adequate concepts of self.
- Teachers and counselors should make every possible attempt to relieve threat whenever it is suspected that a child is handicapped in his perceptions.
- Considering the importance and very role of intelligence and personality in student's life, this study has been undertaken to assess the levels of intelligence and personality in prospective teachers.

## STATEMENT OF THE PROBLEM

"A Study of Intelligence and Personality of Prospective Teachers"

## NEED OF THE STUDY

Individuals differ in mental abilities, as well as in physique and traits of personality. None of us is like any other. Everywhere people influenced by a number of genetic factors and environmental influences differ in behaviour. People differ in varied ways. No two individuals are alike says an adage. Individual differences among the students are a characteristic feature usually observed by a teacher. Some pupils are bright while others are dull; some are able to adapt themselves to new situations easily while others find it difficult to do so; some are quick while others are slow; some learn with little effort while others have to labour hard for it; some are able to solve problems directly and quickly while others fumble with them for a long time and so on and so forth. Though people differ from one another it is only in the extent of the characteristics but not definitely in ability characteristics.

The intellectual development comprehends the development of intellect, mental capabilities, imagination, thinking, emotion, violation and other mental processes. The teacher's duty is to assist the educand in the development of his abilities. What is essential for man, whether young or old, is to live fully, integrally, and that is why our major problem is the cultivation of that intelligence which brings integration. It is really very important that we approach our human problems with an integrated point of view. To be an integrated human being is to understand the entire process of one's own consciousness, both the hidden and the open. We attach great importance to the cultivation of the mind, but inwardly we are insufficient, poor and confused. This living in the intellect is the way of disintegration; for ideas; like beliefs, can never bring people together except in conflicting groups.

As long as we translate experience in terms of the self, of the 'me' and the 'mine', as long as the 'I', the ego, maintains itself through its reactions, experience cannot be freed from conflict, confusion and pain. Freedom comes only when one understands the ways of the self, the experience. It is only when the self, with its accumulated reactions, is not the experience, which experience only takes on an entirely different significance and becomes creation.

Intelligence and Personality are like the two eyes of a man. Even if one is lacking, life becomes meaningless. It is not correct to say that all intelligents possess right personality. Always there are individual differences and different traits responsible for intelligence and personality. Infact intelligence is a part of personality. A prospective teacher can only become a good teacher when he knows about the concepts of intelligence and personality. Though they cannot accelerate maximum amount of intelligence and personality in his students, they can enhance 5 per cent to 10 per cent of intelligence in his students by categorizing them into various groups based on their intelligence and personality enhancement through teacher becoming as a role model to his students. The teacher has to understand each and every individual by letting or dropping himself to the level of the student.

As the prospective teachers have one month teaching internship practice in the nearby schools, when they enter the class, they should be in a position to identify the different categories of students based on their intelligence and personality and progress hand in hand with students by making their instruction easy and understandable to all the students in the class as there will be maximum number of average students and minimum number of dull and bright students. So it is the duty of the teacher to fulfill the needs of all these types of students. Sometimes the teacher has to adjust to the various personalities of the students since some students will be stubborn by nature based on their personality traits, not able to understand the lessons instead of repeated teaching; but the teacher should not loose the heart but try to bring a minute change in the students which will add as milestones to their career. In turn they influence the students in one month in such a way that sometimes they may become role-models to students by their personality. They can transform the introverts to become extroverts by making them to participate in various school programmes and by giving them different activities which involve group work.

Today we see and read in the newspapers that the teachers are ridiculous in punishing their students which may sometimes lead to the physical disability and psychological imbalances on the tender minds of the students which may in the future turn as severe problems which can only be solved by psychotherapist under the careful investigation and medication wherein it may sometimes take years for the patient to become a normal emotionally balanced person.

A teacher can never teach unless he is still learning himself. So it is the utmost responsibility of the teacher to know the concepts of intelligence and personality. The personality of the teacher has a great influence on its students and the first and the foremost quality of a good teacher is that he or she must have an influencing personality not only in words but also in deeds also so that he or she may be a good example to everyone, sometimes moulding himself or herself as to the situation demands.

In our classroom when we function as a teacher, our personality is crucial not only for guiding and directing learning, motivation and interests of our students, but also in tackling the problems and producing an overall orientation for our class. Thus, as human being we daily come into active association with personalities. The end of all knowledge must be building up character. What is education without character and what is character without elementary personal purity. Because of the interest in the problem and to throw some light on this area, the present study is an attempt to ascertain the position in an empirical way.

So, teacher educators, administrators, policy planners and guidance personnel connected with teacher education programmes should think of ways and means of improving and enhancing the levels of intelligence and personality among the teacher trainees so that they can perform still better to improve the qualities among their students when they join the teacher education course.

## SCOPE OF THE STUDY

The present study is confined to the Ranga Reddy district. The sample selected for the study was prospective teachers who were studying in the Colleges of Education and the sample size chosen for the present study was 600 (six hundred ) prospective teachers only.

The variables chosen for the study were gender (male and female), locality (rural and urban), methodology of prospective teachers (arts and science), and educational qualification (graduation and post-graduation).

The other factors that are contributing to the present study are socio-economic status, home background of the students, age, creativity, achievement, aptitude, birth order, type of family whether joint or nuclear family, parent's occupation, interests, adjustment, attitudes (parents as well as the students), motivation, job satisfaction etc., are not taken because of time and money, the researcher has confined the study to four variables only namely, gender, locality, methodology of study and educational qualification of the prospective teachers.

## OBJECTIVES OF THE STUDY

The objectives of the study were:

- To find out the intelligence of prospective teachers.
- To find out the intelligence of male and female prospective teachers.
- To find out the intelligence of rural and urban prospective teachers.
- To find out the intelligence of arts and science prospective teachers.
- To find out the intelligence of graduate and post-graduate prospective teachers.
- To find out the personality of prospective teachers.
- To find out the personality of male and female prospective teachers.

- To find out the personality of rural and urban prospective teachers.
- To find out the personality of arts and science prospective teachers.
- To find out the personality of graduate and post-graduate prospective teachers.
- To find out the correlation between intelligence and personality of prospective teachers.
- To find out the correlation between intelligence and personality of male and female prospective teachers.
- To find out the correlation between intelligence and personality of rural and urban prospective teachers.
- To find out the correlation between intelligence and personality of arts and science prospective teachers.
- To find out the correlation between intelligence and personality of graduate and post-graduate prospective teachers.

## EDUCATIONAL IMPLICATIONS

The present study helps the people and personnel involved in teacher education in reducing the negative aspects of intelligence and personality of prospective teachers if found it in them. It also helps in devising suitable strategies and programmes either to improve or to enhance intelligence and personality. Just as physical training is to be imparted through physical exercise and intellectual through intellectual exercise, even so the training of the spirit is possible only through the exercise of the spirit. And the exercise of the spirit entirely depends on the life and character of thee teacher. If intelligence and personality enhancing strategies and programmes are informed to prospective teachers, they will implement them in classrooms when they become teachers.

Chapter

# 2

# Review of Related Literature

"A man of confidence always commands love and respect, whereas a man of ego always demands and expects love and respect."

— ***Swami Vivekananda***

Any worthwhile research study in any field of knowledge requires an adequate familiarity with the work which has already been done in the same area. A summary of the writings of recognized authorities and of previous research provides evidence that the researcher is familiar with what is already known and what is still unknown and untested. Since effective research is based upon past knowledge, this step helps to eliminate the duplication of what has been done, and provides useful hypotheses and helpful suggestions for significant investigation.

Citing studies that show substantial agreement and those that seem to present conflicting conclusions helps to sharpen and define understanding of existing knowledge in the problem area, provides a background for the research project and makes the researcher aware of the status of the issue. Parading a long list of annotated studies relating to the problem is ineffective and inappropriate. Only those studies that are plainly relevant, competently executed and reported should be included (Bhaskara Rao, D., 1997).

Capitalizing on the review of expert researchers can be fruitful in providing helpful ideas and suggestions. While review articles that summarize related studies are useful, they do not provide a satisfactory substitute for an independent research. Even though the review of related literature is not a substitute for an independent work, it is one of the first steps in the research process. It is a valuable guide to define the problem to recognize its significance, to suggest promising data gathering devices, to appropriate the study design, and sources of data for effective analysis and to arrive at fruitful conclusions. (B.V. Kumari and D.B. Rao, 2000).

The search for related literature is a time consuming process, even though it is necessary, as earlier stated, for a good research work. Hence, this chapter on Review of Related Literature is meant for the study of literature rated to the intelligence and personality.

P.B. Ballard has aptly quipped, "While the teacher tried to cultivate intelligence and psychologists tried to measure intelligence, nobody seemed to know what intelligence was" And, Vernon has given a similar version of the problem when he says: "Although psychologists have been measuring intelligence for over 40 years, they have failed to reach any agreed definition as to what it is they are measuring".

Intelligence is used to denote the powers or capacities of individuals. It differs from one individual to another and from one species to another in terms of the range and depth of the operation. It is the ability to learn, ability to adjust and ability to do abstract thinking and reasoning.

One plays numerous roles in one's life. In fact, the same person exhibits varied behaviour in the same or in identical situations. That is the charisma of personality. When we talk of behaviour implicitly, we talk of personality. No wonder, personality may be considered in terms of the sum total of a man's behaviour unto other people. Or personality includes also attitudes and interests shown consistently.

Personality is the dynamic organization within the individual of those psycho-physical systems that determine his unique adjustment to his environment.

## THEORETICAL PERSPECTIVES

The awareness about intelligence and personality makes the researcher do well in his study.

## INTELLIGENCE

It is not an easy task to depict the nature of intelligence. Since time immemorial, philosophers, poets, scientists, etc., have failed to define God—the source of perennial strength and energy. Similarly, psychologists have failed to give a correct definition of intelligence. Modern psychologists in order to determine the nature of the intelligence have put forward various definitions.

### Meaning of Intelligence

The Dictionary defined intelligence as the capacity to acquire and apply knowledge.

Alfred Binet (1905) defined intelligence as the ability of an individual to direct his behaviour towards a goal. He said that intelligence manifests in purposive direction, active adaptation and conscious correction. It is the ability to take and maintain a given mental set, the capacity to make adaptations for the purpose of attaining the desired end and the power of self criticism.

Ausubel defined intelligence as a general level of cognitive functioning, as reflected in the ability to understand ideas and to utilize abstract symbols (verbal, mathematical or spatial) in the solution of intellectual problems.

Ballard defined intelligence as the relative efficiency of mind measured under similar conditions of knowledge, interest and habituation.

Boring said that intelligence is what intelligence tests test.

Bortelmann said that the patterns of behaviour comprising intelligence are accumulative, acquired, maintained and elaborated by sequential learning experiences.

Buckingham (1921) said that intelligence is the learning ability.

Burt (1949) defined intelligence as inborn, all round efficiency. It is the power of readjustment to relatively novel situations by organizing new psycho-physical coordination.

Calvin defined intelligence as the ability to learn to adjust to one's environment.

According to Charles Darwin and Herbert Spencer, Intelligence has been regarded as an inherent capacity for profiting by experience, adaptation to environment and ability to learn.

Charles Spearman defined intelligence as the analytic and synthetic ability to mind.

David Wechsler (1950) defined intelligence as the aggregate or global capacity of the individual to act purposefully, to think rationally and to deal effectively with his environment.

Dearborn defined intelligence as the capacity to learn or to profit by experience.

E.L. Thorndike (1931) defined intelligence in general as the power of good responses from the point of view of truth or fact.

F.N. Freeman (1937) said that intelligence is represented in behaviour by the capacity of the individual to adjust himself to new situations to solve new problems, to learn.

Gates and others (1955) said that intelligence is a composite organization of abilities to learn, to grasp broad and subtle facts, especially abstract facts, with alertness and accuracy, to exercise mental control and to display flexibility and sagacity in seeking the solution of problems.

G.D. Stoddard (1943) said that intelligence is the ability to undertake activities that are characterized by difficult, complexity, abstraction, economy, adaptiveness to a goal, social value and the emergence of originals and to maintain such activities under conditions that demand a concentration of energy and a resistance to emotional forces.

Goddard defined intelligence as the degree of availability of one's experiences for the solution of immediate problems and the anticipation of future ones.

Henry Garrett (1946) defined intelligence as the abilities demanded in the solution of problems which require the comprehension and use of symbols i.e., words, numbers, diagrams, equations, formulae.

Helm said that intelligent activity consists in grasping the essentials in a given situation and responding appropriately to them.

Howard Gardner defined intelligence as an ability to solve a problem or fashion a product that is valued in one or more cultural settings.

J. Krishnamurthi said that intelligence is much greater than intellect for it is integration of reason and love. Intelligence is the perception of the essential.

J. Piaget (1926) said that intelligence is the adaptation to physical and social environment.

Knight said that intelligence is the capacity for relational constructive thinking, directed to the attainment of some end.

Norman Munn said that intelligence is the flexibility or versatility in the use of symbolic processes.

P.E. Vermon (1927) defined intelligence as all round thinking capacity or mental efficiency. It is what intelligence tests measures.

Pinter always thought of intelligence as the ability of the individual to adapt himself adequately to relatively new situation in life.

Raven said that in order to act intelligently in any situation, a person needs both the necessary information and the capacity to form comparisons and reason by analogy.

Stern (1941) said that intelligence is the general capacity of an individual, consciously to adjust his thinking to new environment. It is a general mental adaptability to new problems and conditions of life.

Terman L.M. (1921) said that an individual is intelligent in proportion as he is able to carry on abstract thinking.

Thouless said that intelligence is the general intellectual capacity.

Wagnon defined intelligence as the capacity to learn and adjust to relatively new and changing conditions.

Webster's New International Dictionary defines intelligence as "the capacity for knowledge and understanding, especially, as applied to the handling of novel situation; the power of meeting a novel situation successfully by adjusting one's behaviour to the total situation".

Wells defined intelligence as the property of recombining our behaviour pattern so as to act better in a novel situation.

William James (1907) defined intelligence as the ability to adjust oneself successfully to a relatively new situation.

William McDougall (1923) said that intelligence is the capacity to improve upon native tendency in the light of past experiences.

William Stern said that intelligence is general adaptability to new problems and conditions of life.

Woodrow said that intelligence is an acquiring capacity.

Woodworth and Marquis said that intelligence means intellect put to use. It is the use of intellectual abilities for handling a situation or accomplishing any task.

## Nature of Intelligence

There is a distinction between the nature of intelligence and its origin or source. The nature of intelligence is how intelligence works in situations calling for it. It is the process working itself out. For purpose of analysis, issues relating to the process can be discussed independently of issues relating to the origin of intelligence, although obviously the two cannot be regarded as unrelated. The two most prominent theories of the nature of intelligence are that: (i) it is the capacity to learn; and (ii) it is ability to act with foresight.

### *Intelligence as capacity to learn*

Psychologists who think of intelligence as capacity to learn have advanced numerous competing ideas concerning its exact nature. Alfred Binet (1857-1911), a French psychologist opinioned that intelligence was unitary in the sense that each person had a certain amount which could be used for any purpose; it was a general ability to learn. Accordingly, if a person did better in one field of activity than in another, it was not due to any fundamental variation in intelligence relative to the two fields, but to factors such as learning, interest and motivation. Lewis Terman (1877-1956), an American psychologist, saw intelligence as ability to do abstract thinking, an ability which can be directed towards repairing an automobile motor just as well as towards solving a problem in quantum mechanics. William Stern (1871-1938), a German professor, regarded intelligence as adaptability to new problems and conditions of life. Charles E. Spearmen (1863-1945), an English psychologist, thought that two factors contributed to every intelligent act: g, a general factor operative in all situations, and s, a specific factor operative only in situations where that specific factor is involved. Edward L. Thorndike divided intelligence into mechanical, social and abstract. Hence they have constructed the nature of intelligence as capacity to form new responses to stimuli in rapid and accurate manner in situations which so permit.

### *Intelligence as ability to act with foresight*

When one acts with foresight, he looks ahead; he tries to anticipate the consequences of acting in a particular way. He makes forecasts regarding the outcome of alternative lines of action. These forecasts are based upon experience. For example, if experience has taught a person that although rattlesnake bites are not usually fatal they do make one very ill; he will behave very cautiously in rattlesnake country so as to avoid getting bitten. In difficult situations they are able to test their hunches or hypotheses intellectually so that in their overt behaviour they appear to do a minimum of fumbling and they choose the correct act almost instantly. With an increase in age and experience, a mature person may show increased flexibility of behaviour and imagination. It harmonizes well with a relativistic, cognitive-field psychology, it does not square with the notion that intelligence is based upon the capacity to form and retain connections in the nervous system.

## Sources of Intelligence

Where does intelligence come from? What causes one person to act with high intelligence and another low? Three positions which may be taken on this matter are that: (i) intelligence is genetic endowment; (ii) intelligence is a product of learning; and (iii) intelligence is a function of interaction of self and environment.

### *Intelligence as genetic endowment*

Intelligence bears a one-to-one relation to the quality of genes which determine the structure and functioning of the organic-neutral-endocrine system. Intelligence is a function of the way an organism is put together. In other words, intelligence hinges on physical structure. This outlook harmonizes well with a psychology that emphasizes physiology as a determiner of what can be achieved. The two traits crucial to intelligence—complexity and modifiability of the nervous system—supposedly were transmitted from parents to offspring. Thus connectionist psychologists reasoned that intelligence, like other physical traits, is determined by physical inheritance and that its level is constant for each individual just as the colour of his eyes and skin is constant.

### *Intelligence as a product of learning*

All people except those who are obviously defective have the same potential at birth. Accordingly, the intelligence they achieve stems from opportunities for learning which they have had. Intelligence is, at least in large measure, learned. Some of the studies of changes of IQ in individuals give support to hypothesis that intelligence is learned rather than inborn.

### *Intelligence as a function of interaction*

Intelligence is capacity to act with foresight, i.e., to assess accurately the consequences of a proposed action, and then goes on to by-pass completely the issue of whether intelligence is inherited or learned. Intelligence is a product of the interaction of a human self and its perceived environment.

To summarize and restate the position, intelligence is a product of the interaction of a person and his perceived, i.e., psychological and environment. But, we can attribute no particular portion of intelligence to heredity and no particular portion to environment.

## Theories of Intelligence

The theories of intelligence propagated from time to time have tried to answer what are the different components or elements of intelligence. Some of the theories of intelligence are as follows.

### *Unitary theory or Monarchic theory*

Intelligence is regarded as an adaptiveness which enables a creation to adjust itself to changing environment. This is a popular view which regards intelligence as a single unit or a unitary faculty that determines the level of man's achievement in any intellectual enterprise he may undertake. An inborn all round mental efficiency is a sign of intelligence.

### *Spearman's two factor theory or Eclectic theory*

Charles Spearman thought that two factors contribute to every intelligent act: g, a general factor operative in all situations and s, specific factor operative only in situations where that specific factor is involved. Thus, he thought that a person's capacity to act in any situation depends both upon his general capacity and upon the special capacity involved in that particular act. To illustrate: a person might have a fairly mediocre general intelligence but a very high order of special capacity in, say, music.

### *Group factor theory*

Factor analysis and correlations were suggestive of possible main factors which surpassed even the multifactor theory. Thurston was the prominent propagator. He found correlations of appropriately 60 separate tests and differentiated nine factors: (*a*) Verbal factor 'V' concerns with comprehension of verbal relations, words and ideas (*b*) Spatial factor 'S' involved in any task in which the subject manipulates an object imaginatively in space (*c*) Numerical factor 'N' is ability to do numerical calculations rapidly and accurately (*d*) Memory factor 'M' involves the ability to memorize quickly (*e*) Word fluency factor 'W' involved whenever the subject is asked to think of the isolated words at a rapid rate (*f*) Reasoning 'R' found in tasks that require the subject to discover a rule or principle (*g*) Inductive reasoning 'IR' : Deductive reasoning 'DR' (*h*) Perceptual factor 'P' is the ability to perceive what is exactly there and (*i*) Problem-solving ability factor 'PS' is the ability to perceive the problem and solve it.

### *Anarchic theory or Multifactor theory*

An American psychologist E.L Thorndike developed multifactor theory. Intelligence, according to him is forming a number of actual or potential specific connections between specific stimuli and responses. From the point of view of the tasks performed by people intelligence can be understood as concrete intelligence-ability to deal with concrete aspects, abstract intelligence-ability to deal with abstract phenomena and social intelligence-ability to deal with people and relations. He distinguishes four attributes of intelligence: (*a*) Level refers to task difficulty in which the test items are arranged in sequential order of increasing difficulty determining the level or altitude of intelligence; (*b*) Range or width refers to a number of tasks, at any degree of difficulty, which we can solve. It is the breadth of experience represented by items of equal difficulty; (*c*) Area means the total number of situations at each level. It is the summation of all ranges at each level of intelligence; and (*d*) Speed is the rapidity with which we can respond to test items. Speed and altitude are positively correlated.

### *G.H. Thomson's sampling theory*

It assumes that the mind is made of many independent bonds or elements. This theory seems to combine various theoretical view points: (*i*) It appears to be similar to Thorndike's multifactor theory except that he concedes to the practical usefulness of a concept like 'g'; (*ii*) Thomson seems to maintain that the concept of group factor 'G' is of equal practical usefulness.

Thus any mental operation or task involves three kinds of basic factors: (*a*) Spearman's general factor 'g'—common to all tasks; (*b*) Group factor 'G'—common to the tasks belonging to specific group; and (*c*) Specific factor $s_1$, $s_2$, $s_3$ etc.—very specific to the task.

### *Vernon's Hierarchical theory*

Vernon (1950) developed analytic view of organization of intelligence on the basis of empirical data. He suggests that intelligence tests measure an overall 'G' factor as well as two main types of mental abilities, Ved: Verbal, numerical and educational and K.M.: Practical, mechanical, spatial and physical. These two major factors can be divided into minor group factors such as mechanical and manual. These minor factors can be further divided into various Specific factors.

It accounts for the proliferation of apparently conflicting findings and multiplicity of ability factors. Different kinds of factors operating at different levels and the tests serve different purposes in assessment and prediction.

### *Guilford's Structure of Intellect*

The Guilford's Structure of Intellect or Theory of Intellect has 150 factors or specific factors of intelligence and 16 categories of intelligence, all come under 3 heads namely contents (5), operations (5) and products (6). It is in the form of a cube i.e., 5 × 5 × 6 = 150.

1. Contents refer to the nature of information obtained in the environment i.e., the information we get from the environment, the kind or material of content to which the person responds and the type of information available in the environment. There are five kinds of material namely: (*a*) Visual-information in the visual form; (*b*) Auditory-information in auditory form; (*c*) Symbolic-information in the form of signs which have no significance by themselves; (*d*) Semantic-

information in the form of meanings; and (*e*) Behavioural non-verbal information used in human interactions.

2. Operations refer to what one has to do with the environment i.e., it includes the act of thinking. Mental operations are classified into five major groups of intellectual abilities: (*a*) Cognition—discovery, rediscovery or recognition of information is the most important information operation in learning process; (*b*) Memory—retention and recall of what is recognized. It is a primary mental process; (*c*) Divergent production—searching for all possible situations and varieties of thinking. It is also a component of creativity which shows the relationship between intelligence and creativity; (*d*) Convergent production—generation of information from the given information. Conventionally accepted and best outcomes are emphasized. The given information fully determines the response; and (*e*) Evaluation—making decisions or judgements concerning criteria as to goodness, correctness, suitability or adequacy of what we know, what we remember and what we produce in productive thinking.
3. Product is the result of an operation upon the content which produces the final result. When a certain operation is applied on certain kind of content, six kinds of products may be resulting factors: (*a*) Units—they are segregated wholes or it is a small portion of a big unit; (*b*) Classes—a set of objects with similar properties; (*c*) Relations—some kind of connection between two things; (*d*) Systems—patterns of organizations of inter-dependent and interacting parts; (*e*) Transformation—a change or revision of one's knowledge; and (*f*) Implication—a prediction or expectation from a given information.

Thus Guilford structurally presented five categories of mental operations working on five kinds of contents giving rise to six kinds of products. The total outcome of 150 factors i.e., by 5 contents × 5 operations × 6 products is traced.

### *Gardner's Theory of Multiple Intelligence*

According to this theory intelligence is not a single factor. It is a combination of different abilities developed autonomously according to heredity and environment. Gardner called the eight types of intelligence independent as each intelligence is a relatively autonomous intellectual potential which is capable of functioning independently of the others.

Linguistic Intelligence is the ability to read, write and communicate with words having components like syntax, semantics and pragmatics. The best examples are authors, journalists, poets, orators, comedians and other professionals like lawyers.

Logico-Mathematical Intelligence is the ability to reason, calculate and to think things in a logical, systematic manner. These types of abilities and skills are highly developed in engineers, scientists, economists, accountants, detectives and the members of legal profession.

Visual Spatial Intelligence is concerned with the abilities, talents and skills involving the representation and manipulation of spatial configuration and relationship. Architects, artists, sculptors, sailors, photographers and strategic planners rely on it in their own ways.

Musical Intelligence is the ability to make or compose music to sing well, or understand and appreciate music. One's capacity for pitch discrimination, sensitivity to rhythm, texture and timber, ability to hear themes in music and abilities pertaining to the field of music.

Bodily-Kinesthetic Intelligence is the ability to use body skillfully to solve problems, create products or present ideas and emotions, the ability displayed for athletic pursuits, artistic pursuits such as dancing and acting, or in building and construction and the ability to perform skillfully and purposeful movements. Lancers, athletes, surgeons etc., demonstrate it to high degree.

Intra-personal Intelligence is the ability to know himself, his own cognitive strengths, styles and mental functioning as well as one's feelings, range of emotions and skills to utilize one's fund of knowledge in practical situations. Philosophers, yogis and saints demonstrate it.

Inter-personal Intelligence is the ability to understand and work with others, to relate with other people, display empathy and to notice their motives and goals. Teachers, sales people, politicians and religious leaders possess this type of intelligence.

Naturalistic Intelligence is the ability to recognize flora and fauna, to make other consequential distinctions in the natural world, and to use this ability productively in farming, in biological science and hunting. Farmers, botanists, conservationists, biologists and environmentalists would display this.

## Testing of Intelligence

Intelligence is tested in terms of Intelligence Quotient (IQ). It means a child's mental age divided by its chronological age multiplied by 100.

$$\text{Intelligence Quotient} = \frac{\text{Mental age}}{\text{Chronological age}} \times 100$$

Mental age is an index of intelligence which means that a given child's performance in a contest is like the average performance in the same test of children of a given chronological age.

Chronological age is the physical age of a person, counted from the date and time of his birth. It is counted in terms of years, months and hours. Suppose a nine years old child has a mental age of eleven years, his IQ will be 122. IQ is not the quantity of a person's intelligence, all tests do not yield an identical IQ and IQ changes at least once every three years.

Even when a person is examined by the same test a number of times, then IQ shows a change. The difference differs from test to test. The IQ of any child does not remain constant. In fact it registers a very wide change. IQ is the result both of the heredity and environment. Thus a change in environment may change IQ. According to Garret the good and bad environment show a difference of 10 points.

There is a possibility of increase in IQ along with a rise in the social and economic status and a possibility of increase in IQ with degradation. It generally remains constant from 5 years to 14 years of age. The mental level develops gradually. Many scientific researchers have made it clear that there is no invariable relation between IQ and success in school work. But in children with a higher IQ there is a possibility of success in school work.

Binet's classification of Intelligence Quotient according to range of IQ and class are as: below IQ 20—idiots, IQ between 20 to 39.9—imbeciles, IQ between 40 to 59.9—moron's, IQ between 60 to 69.9—borderline, IQ between 70 to 79.9—very backward, IQ between 80 to 98.9—backward, IQ between 99 to 109.9—average or normal, IQ between 110 to 119.9—superior, IQ between 120 to 129.9—very superior, IQ between 130 to 139.9—extra-ordinary and IQ 140 and above—genius.

## Classification of Intelligence Tests

Intelligence tests can be grouped under three heads—verbal tests, non-verbal tests and performance tests depending upon the contents of the tests. Some intelligence tests depending require the use of language or verbal ability, the ability to read, write or understand words. A test which requires the use of verbal ability of the subjects is called a verbal test. Tests of intelligence which requires no use of language in its administration or in the subject's answers which are non-language in character are known as non-verbal tests. Non-verbal tests may be pictorial or performance type.

### *Verbal tests*

*Information:* The range of individual information is an indication of his intellectual capacity. Intelligentsias have broader interests, more curiosity and seek mental stimulation. It consists of items to test the subject's knowledge about the world and its culture. Example, How many weeks are there in a year?

*Comprehension:* It is a test of common sense, practical judgement and logical thinking. The subject must comprehend what is involved in the situation and give answers to problems presented. It comprises of 25 items. Example, Why should people pay taxes? Why are coins made of steel?

*Digits forward and digits backward:* When digits are repeated forward, the series includes from 3 to 9, for backward repetition of 3 to 8 digits are considered.

*Arithmetic reasoning:* Items are designed to test the mental alertness. The problems are of an increasing degree of difficulty.

*Similarities:* 12 items were designed to test identification or likeness between different objects, ability to find the similarity by looking in one glance. Example, In what way is a piano and a violin alike?

*Vocabulary:* 40 words ranging in difficulty from very common ones to very rare ones are used. It is one of the most valuable types of material used in deriving an index of a person's general mental ability. Qualitative differences in word definitions have clinical value and educational significance in trying to reveal the nature of an individual's thought processes, feelings, emotions and values.

### *Non-verbal tests*

*Digit symbol test:* Some rectangles with a digit in the upper half and a symbol in the lower half will be given which is a key. Then, it is followed by some more rectangles in which only the numerals are given. Appropriate symbols are to be inserted in lower half. Speed and accuracy of performance are measured here.

*Picture completion test:* Some cards containing drawings, with an important part missing. The subject has to name the missing part. Basic perceptual and conceptual abilities are measured.

*Picture arrangement test:* It consists of some sets of pictures. Each series is presented to the subject in a disarranged manner. When the pictures of a set are placed in the correct sequence, they tell a story, this test measures a person's ability to comprehend and evaluate the total situation without the use of language.

*Block design test:* Some identical cubes are utilized, of which some or all of them are used to copy the given designs. It involves visual analysis and synthesis. It is the ability of an individual to arrange these blocks.

*Object assembly test:* It includes 'figure form boards' that represent familiar objects, each cut into several parts which the subject assembles into the whole. Perception of parts and their reconstruction into a meaningful whole are required.

### *Performance tests of intelligence*

Performance tests are usefully administered to those who have very poor verbal ability or no mastery over any language. These tests are also useful in case of deaf and dumb or blind children. In these tests, the person is required to perform some act or do some practical work. The subject may be asked to trace a maze or fit forms into a form-board. Pinter Peterson Scale of Performance Tests needs special mention in this regard.

Originally, the test was based on fifteen form board test meant for children from four to sixteen years. A shorter version of the test's scale was issued in 1937 by Pinter and Mildreth. A few other performance tests are :

(*i*) *Porteus Maze Test* used for children as well as adults. The subject is required to trace the shortest path from the entrance to the exit of the maze, without ever lifting the pencil from the paper.

(*ii*) *Man Drawing Test* in which the subject is required to draw as best as possible a man on the paper. The scoring is done in terms of the important parts shown in the drawing.

(*iii*) *Dr. Alexander's Group of Performance Tests* is a combination of three tests. These tests are:

(*a*) Koh's Block Design Test consists of sixteen coloured inch cubes and ten designs painted in the same colours on the card board. The subject is required to arrange the cubes in such a way that the design may be reproduced.

(*b*) The Cube Construction Test consists of three parts, each comprising a set of inch cubes. The subject is required to construct a bigger model block with the help of inch cubes.

(*c*) The Pass Along Test in which the subject is required to reproduce, in a given time, a given design by passing along, not lifting the wooden pieces, coloured red or blue, which are presented in a standardized order, in a wooden frame.

(*iv*) *Culture Fair Test* is used to delete the influence of culture in the test items.

(*v*) *Raven's Progressive Matrices Test* devised in 1938 was reprinted in 1940, 1947 and again revised in 1952 and 1956. There are three types of progressive matrices tests namely Standard Progressive Matrices test, Coloured Progressive Matrices and Advanced Progressive Matrices Test.

Standard Progressive Matrices test consists of five bits ABCDE. In each of these sets there are 12 problems. In each set the problems are arranged in order of difficulty. They cover the entire range of intellectual development, from childhood to adulthood. This test consists of logically designed graded series of patterns serving to measure the innate educative ability and educative intelligence. Each of the five sets in this test involves a different principle but all require the subject to supply a missing part to a design by choosing one of six possible inserts. Themes of these successive sets of subsets are continuous patterns, figure analogies, progressive alteration of patterns, permutation of figures and reduction of figures into constituent parts.

Coloured Progressive Matrices is used to test young children and old people for clinical work and people suffering from disability or intellectually backward.

Advanced Progressive Matrices Test is meant for the people of above 11 years, who have more than average intellectual ability.

Consequently the verbal and non-verbal tests are capable of further sub-division into two classes—individual and group. Individual tests are conducted on a single individual at a time whereas group tests are conducted on many individuals or group of individuals at a time. Thus, finally there are four types of intelligence tests namely verbal individual intelligence test, non-verbal individual, verbal group and non-verbal group intelligence tests.

### *Verbal Individual Intelligence Tests*

These are intelligence tests given to individuals, or in other words they are meant to test the intelligence of individuals.

Language finds adequate use in them. Binet Simon tests and the various revisions are all included in this classification.

### *Non-verbal Individual Intelligence Tests*

It is quite apparent from the above example that in verbal tests, the child's knowledge of language is more in demand and therefore the use of these tests is limited to students or literate individuals as these tests cannot be used in the case of illiterate individuals as these tests involve an extensive use of language which fails a medium to ensure the individual differences between the illiterates. Consequently illiterate individuals are tested with the help of Non-verbal Individual Intelligence tests. These tests involve the least possible uses of the linguistic ability and are similarly almost unaffected by knowledge derived from books. Performance Intelligence Tests are an example of the non-verbal individual intelligence test. According to Munn, "The word performance is usually applied to tests which require a minimum use of understanding and language." Thus, these tests make use of items requiring responses and not language and these tests can be applied to children, illiterates, feeble-minded individuals as well as foreigners.

(*a*) There is concept learning on the basis of primary stimulus generalization.

(*b*) Concept learning depends largely upon discrimination learning.

(*c*) Concept learning involves transfer of learning on the basis of symbolic mediating responses.

The first two types of concept learning are those based upon primary stimulus generalization and those based on discrimination. The third category includes only those tasks in which the concept could not be attained except by means of symbolically mediating learning. This type of concept learning introduces a host of sources, of individual differences variants that are not apt to play a prominent role in similar types of learning.

According to Jensen, "Mediated concept learning will be affected to a large extent by transfer of learning from the subject's past experience. The subject's verbal repertoire, the structure of severable associative network, the strength of the subject's tendency to make verbal responses to non-verbal stimuli and other such processes which are a mixture of nature and nature will figure among the main determinants of individual differences in concept of learning of the mediated variety." Finally, distinction must be made between tasks that involve only concept identification, without any learning whatever being tapped by the task and tasks that involve learning parameters. It is generally easier to measure individual differences in status. However, Jensen was concerned with individual differences in processes. He maintained equilibrium.

Piaget made sensory motor adaptations in the psychological development of his own three children. He explained the successive coordination as providing the basic thought, the hierarchical nature of intelligence and intellectual concepts. Following the six stages of sensory motor development the sensory motor systems of infant became internalized as imitative imagery combines with imitated vocal signs of early languages. These are modified in the accommodations demanded by communications into intuitive regulations. He shows maximum dissonant with the notion that the laws of organization are constant in the course of human development. According to him the systems of behaviour and thought are seen to develop into more complex hierarchical organizations.

The uses of these tests are instructions can be given clearly, no scope of malpractice, motivation can be given and other behavioural characteristics can be observed. The limitations of Individual Tests are difficulty of time since only one person can be tested at a time, need for experienced examiners, tests are expensive and individuals may not perform well due to stress.

### *Verbal Group Intelligence Tests*

All the people in the group are given the same directions and have to perform the same activities. Even the score of the result of group intelligence tests is calculated by machines thus independent upon the necessity of skilled examiners, accompanied by an economy of time.

An excellent example of group intelligence tests is afforded by the Army alpha and beta tests, which were evolved during the World War I in order to test the American soldiers. For example, it revealed separately the feeble-minded, men capable of becoming skilled specialists, men capable of becoming officers, men needing some training, etc.

The limitations of Verbal Group tests are difficulties relating to co-operation in test, difficulty related to the balance of the subject, difficulty related to the ease of the subject and possibility of cheating by the subject.

### *Non-Verbal Group Intelligence Tests*

In non-verbal group intelligence tests the examiners have to explain to the examinees even the simplest directions which are also demonstrated as far as possible. All this is done to make the least possible use of language. Many individual's can be tested at a time, time saving, economical and students can freely perform the tests without any stress. One of the best examples is Cattell's Culture free test. Some psychologists do not give credence to these non-verbal tests in their role of measuring intelligence of the subjects while on the other hand some psychologists consider them to be better than verbal tests.

The truth is that even if non-verbal group intelligence tests are not more important than verbal tests, they are certainly not less important than these tests. Some of their peculiarities are comparison of various human groups, the testing of illiterate soldiers and the linguistic ability is very low in the case of children and consequently the verbal group intelligence tests cannot be given to them.

## PERSONALITY

In this world, various things are understood and realized, but it is very difficult to express them through words. Similarly to express personality through words is a very difficult, though not impossible. The derivation of the word 'Personality' from 'Persona' indicates that the personality can be measured from the external traits as well. From the Layman's point of view, personality means those qualities which cast their influence on others. From sociological view point "Personality is the integration of all traits which determine the role of the status of the person in society, personality might be, therefore as, social effectiveness". Personality is known by the conduct, behaviour, activities, movements and everything else concerning the individual. It is the way of responding to the environment, the way in which an individual adjusts with the external environment.

Personality trait is the ultimate reality in the psychological organization. It is free from the observer, since it is given in the mental structure. Traits are different from habits though both are determinant propensities.

### Meaning of Personality

Allport, C.W (1937) defined personality as the dynamic organization within the individual of those psycho-physical systems that determine his unique adjustment to his environment.

Boring said that personality is an individual's typical or consistent adjustment to his environment.

Brown, W. (1946) said that personality is the total differentiation which the individual makes by incorporating the inherited and acquired powers to stimulate and to activate the imagination of others in art, science and public affairs and also to live in and partake of a super-individual and super-temporal world of values.

Burgess E.W. said that personality is the integration of all traits which determine the role and status of the person in society.

Cattle, R.B. (1967) said that personality is that which permits a prediction of what a person will do in a given situation.

Dashiell, J.F. (1929) defined personality as the sum total of behaviour trends manifested in his social adjustments.

Eysenck, H.J. (1947) said that personality is a stable and enduring combination of a persons various physical and mental aspects.

Guilford, J.P. (1967) said that an individual's personality is his unique pattern of traits-a trait is any distinguishable relatively enduring way in which one individual differs from another.

Fredenburgh in his book, the psychology of personality and adjustment, tried to synthesize all definitions and observed, "Personality is a stable system of complex characteristics by which the life pattern of the individual may be identified".

J.B. Watson (1924) defined personality as the sum of activities that can be discovered by actual observation over a long enough period of time to give reliable information.

Jones, A.J. (1930) said that personality consists of the way you look, the way you dress, the way you talk, the way you walk, the way you act, the skill with which you do things and your health.

Kemph defined personality as the integration of that system of habits that represent one individual's characteristic adjustment to his environment.

Kolb, L. said that each individual's characteristically recurring patterns of behaviour are known as personality.

Lewin, Kurt (1935) defined personality as a dynamic totality of systems.

McClelland defined personality as the most adequate conceptualization of a person's behaviour in all its detail.

McDougal, J.W. (1932) defined personality as a synthetic unity of all mental features and functions in their interplay.

Morton Prince (1914) defined personality as the sum total of all biological innate dispositions, impulses, tendencies, aptitudes and instincts of the individual and the dispositions and tendencies acquired by experience.

Munn defined personality as the most characteristic integration of an individual's structure, modes of behaviour, interests, attitudes, capacities, abilities and aptitudes.

Murphy, G. (1933) defined personality as a unitary mode of adjustment in relation to which each specific activity is not to be taken into consideration.

Ogden, R.M. (1926) said that personality is the expression of man's inner life. Character is the expression of what he does or achieves.

Prince M. said that personality is the sum total of all the biological innate dispositions, impulses, tendencies, appetites and instincts of the individual and the acquired disposition and tendencies.

Shaffer said that personality consists of observable behaviour which is individualistic and intrinsic. Personality is defined as an individual's typical or consistent adjustment to his environment.

Sullivan said that personality is the relatively enduring pattern of recurrent interpersonal situations which characterize a human life.

Warren, H.C. (1935) said that personality is the entire mental organization of a human being at any stage of development.

William Healy regards personality as an integrated system of habitual adjustments to the environment, particularly to the social environment.

Woodworth defined personality as the study of the sum total of the behaviour of an individual. It includes not only the physical, emotional behaviour and intellectual aspects, but their organized patterns.

Valentine defined personality as the sum total of innate and acquired dispositions.

## Nature of Personality

- Personality is a whole rather than the sum of parts. Just as the various parts of the automobile mechanically joined do not enable it to perform its function, so is the case with the various ingredients of personality.
- Personality implies an integration of various traits. The integration of various traits results into a 'distinct whole' which is known by the name of personality of an individual.
- Personality represents a unique integration of traits so as to differentiate one person from another on the basis of this very quality. The unique way, in which we laugh or smile, weep or cry, talk or lecture, greet or salute our elders, becomes the watermark of our personality.
- Personality is the result of both heredity and environment. It is the outcome of the dynamic interaction of an organism with his soul, psychological and physical environments. Heredity is represented by 'genes' and environment is represented by any 'stimulation' minus genes.

- Personality is composed of traits which are by and large learned or acquired. By the time we become a mature personality, the contribution of learning is so prominent that we often misinterpret personality as equivalence of learning.
- Each personality can be identified with some 'motive' force. The concept of motives as 'drives'—the pushing force, the incentives—the pulling force and the ego-involved, all become relevant in understanding the formation of our personality from early infancy to the adulthood.

## Determinants of Personality

Some important determinants of personality are genetic factors, physiological determinants such as ductless glands, nervous system, emotions, psychological factors, and social and cultural factors that mould personality. If the factors other than heredity are termed environmental they include family factors, school factors and social factors.

The endocrine glands or ductless glands, pancreas, thyroid gland, adrenal gland, pituitary glands and the gonads influence the personality of an individual. The behaviour towards different individuals is modified to some extent according to their physical structure. This difference in behaviour makes a change in the personality. Chromosomes and gene structures obtained at the time of conception determine a number of other characteristics. The family climate, the nature of the members of the family and the way of interaction among them and their influence on the growing children, the atmosphere at school and in classroom, curricular subjects, co-curricular activities, parent-teacher interactions, influence of mass media-T.V., films, print media; social, cultural and political environment and religious harmony, all determine the personality of an individual.

The development of personality, though continuous, precedes through certain crisis situations. Sometimes, these crises are brought about by maturational processes like teething or pubertal changes, sometimes by internal bodily processes like gestation or increased activity of adrenal glands, sometimes by certain social situations like marriage or death, and sometimes by certain cultural pressures like retirement. Most often, a crisis involves more than any one factor.

## Structure of Personality

The search for the nature of personality will be rather incomplete if we do not mention some important theories of personality which attempt to explain the very structure of personality. This helps us in classifying the people into some categories according to their personality characteristics and gives a base for the assessment of their personality. The theories of personality, in general, can be classified into four broad categories according to their modes of approach.

The theories which adopt Type-approach: The view points of Hippocrates, Kretschmer, Sheldon and Jung belong to this category. They hold that human personalities can be classified into few clearly defined types and each person can be put in one of the other types according to his personality traits.

The theories which adopt trait-approach: Worth mentioning in this category is Cattell's theory of personality. This approach believes in the mathematical analysis and quantification of the personality constituents and helps in the prediction of human behaviour in a particular situation.

The theories which adopt type as well as trait approach: Eysenck's theory of personality belongs to this category. He goes a step ahead to the approach adopted by Cattell. He does not only mention the personality traits for assessing one's personality but also tries to give definite personality types.

The theories which adopt developmental approach are the theories which try to explain the growth and development of personality. The Psycho-analytical theory of Freud and theory of Individual Psychology by Adler come into this category.

### *(A) Trait Approaches*

Hippocrates classification tried to classify all human beings into four characteristic groups according to their temperaments as: (*i*) *Choleric*—active but irritable and emotionally weak but bodily strong; (*ii*) *Phlegmatic*—happy but lazy and emotionally strong but bodily weak; (*iii*) *Sanguinic*—excessive blood, cheerful energetic and optimistic, and bodily strong and emotionally stable; and (*iv*) *Melancholic*—no energy and no happiness, pessimistic and emotionally as well as bodily weak.

Kretschmer's classification classified all human beings into certain biological types according to their physical structure and has allotted definite personality characteristics associated with each physical make-up as follows: (*i*) Pyknic's have excess fat in their body. They are happy, jolly, easy going, sociable and good natured and mostly seen in social activities; (*ii*) Athletic's have muscular body build. They are good in athletics and emotionally balanced. They take risks and do adventures, energetic, optimistic and adjustable; and (*iii*) Leptosomatic's are very lean, thin and bony. They are pessimistic, unsociable, reserved, shy and sensitive.

Sheldon classified human beings into certain types according to their physical structures and attached certain temperamental characteristics to them as: (*i*) Endomorphic person having highly developed viscera but weak somatic structure like Kretschmer's Pyknic type. They are easy going, sociable and affectionate; (*ii*) Mesomorphic person having balanced development of viscera and somatic structure like Kretschmer's Athletic type. They are craving for muscular activity, self assertive, loves risk and adventure; and (*iii*) Ectomorphic person who has weak somatic structure as well as undeveloped viscera like Kretschmer's Leptosomatic type. They are pessimistic, unsociable and reserved.

Carl Gustav Jung has divided all the human beings basically into two distinct types namely introverts and extroverts according to their social participation and the interest which they take in social activities. The introverts are unsociable, careful, lonely, thinking type, good writers, poets and painters, maintain poor social relations, suffer for themselves but do not express outside, rigid, followers, reserved, sensitive, pessimistic and very silent. On the other hand, the extroverts are sociable, easy going, live with people, acting and expressing type, good orators, good in maintaining social relations and at social activities, express their ideas outside, flexible, leaders, optimistic and balanced and controlled. Jung has been criticized for explaining these extreme categories only. So later he has given Ambiverts who have some of the qualities of extroverts and some of the qualities of introverts. These people lie between introverts and extroverts.

### *(B) Developmental Approach*

Freud's anatomy of personality is built around the concept of Id, Ego and Super ego. Each of these aspects of personality is related with the other two. (*i*) Id is the raw, savage and immortal basic stuff of a man's personality. It consists of such ambitions, desires, tendencies and appetites of an individual as are guided by pleasure seeking principle. It knows no laws, follows no rules and considers only the satisfaction of its needs and appetites; (*ii*) Ego acts as a policeman to check the unlawful activities of the Id. It is the executive unit with Veto powers. It follows the principle of reality and acts with intelligence in controlling, selecting and deciding what appetites have to be satisfied and in which way they are to be satisfied; and (*iii*) Super ego is the ethical moral arm of the personality. It is idealistic and does not care for realities. Perfection is its goal rather than pleasure. It is a decision making body which decides what is bad or good, virtue or vice according to the standard of society, which it accepts. All the above personality constituents—Id, Ego and Super ego are inter-related. Although each has its own function yet it can never exist alone.

Adler opposed the Freudian's structure of personality. He told that sex is not the life energy or the centre of human activities. Actually, power motive is the centre urge. Human beings are motivated by the urge to be important or powerful. All of us strive towards superiority but each strives in a different way. He named it as 'style of life'. Therefore, what kind of personality one possesses can be understood by studying his style of life i.e. the goals of life he has set for himself and the way of striving for achieving these goals. In this way he gave birth to individual approach in the study of personality pattern and maintained that there are no definite personality types or classes. Each individual is a unique pattern in himself because everybody has definite goals and style of his life.

### *(C) Trait Approach*

*Cattell's view:* For giving the structure of personality an empirical and scientific base the trait approach was adopted by R.B. Cattell. It intends to give certain specific dimensions to personality so that the human behaviour, related to a particular situation can be predicted. Cattell has adopted factor analysis as a technique for this work. (*a*) Cattell began by attempting to obtain a complete list of all possible human behaviours. He collected a list of 171 words related with personality and called these as Trait-elements; (*b*) the next step is to find out how they are related. He found that each trait element correlated high with some of others and low with some. In this way he managed to form some specific groups and called them Surface Traits; (*c*) Again he went on examining these surface traits in terms of their Interco relations. There was overlapping. The removal of such overlapping gave him desired basic dimensions which he called Source Traits; and (*d*) after obtaining source traits (which were

15 in numbers) he tried to use them to predict behaviour employing what is called a specification equation.

Response = $s_1 T_1 + s_2 T_2 + \ldots\ldots\ldots s_n T_n$

In this way the response or behaviour of an individual is predicted from the degree to which he exhibits each source trait (T) modified by the importance of the trait for that response(s).

*Eysenck's view:* He gave more specification by grouping traits into definite types. Hence his approach is trait cum type approach. There are four levels of behaviour organization: (*i*) At the lowest level we have specification responses. They grow out of particular responses to any single act. For example 'blushing' is a specific response; (*ii*) At the second level we have habitual responses. If the individual reacts in the similar fashion when the same situation reoccurs, we get habitual responses. For example not easily picking up friendship, hesitant to talk to strangers etc. are habitual responses; (*iii*) At the third level we have organization of habitual acts into traits. The behaviour acts which have similarities are said to belong to one group called trait. In the above examples the habitual responses give birth to a group or trait called 'Shyness'; and (*iv*) At the fourth level we have organization of traits into general type. A type is defined as a group of correlated traits. The traits which are similar in nature give birth to a definite type of trait. A person now can be classified as Introvert if he has traits as described at level (*iii*), habits and habit systems as described at level (*ii*), and responds specifically as described at level (*i*). Eysenck has given the following distinct types: introversion, extroversion, neuroticism and psychotism. He has also tried to link different traits and characteristics with each of these types.

## Estimate of Trait Theories

The following three observations of Ernest R. Hilgard summarize the estimate of trait theories: (*a*) The trait approach to describing personality is straight forward one and lends itself readily to experimentation; (*b*) The trait profile that emerges from the scores of an individual is not an adequate description of his personality, even though it may be a true one. When behaviour is broken down into traits, we have no way of knowing how the traits are ordered in the goal seeking behaviour of the individual. Thus, the trait profile, while it tells something about personality patterning, is not dynamic enough to show the interrelationships of the traits in the individual; and (*c*) An individual's traits are his ways of behaving under environmental provocation, and their existence depends upon the inter-action between person and environment. There is some objection to assigning traits to an individual as though they were something he possessed. He does not possess shyness or forwardness, he acts and feels shy under some circumstance and acts forward and does not feel shy under other circumstances.

## Nature of Personality Theory

A theory of personality implies a set of assumptions relevant to human behaviour derived from empirical phenomena. It is an economical way of summarizing the various facts and their relationships in respect of personality. The nature of a personality theory may be indicated by examining the various theories of personality. The main groups of personality theories are: type theories, developmental theories and trait theories. A close scrutiny of these theories may reveal the following: (*a*) Personality theories show a lack of explicitness. They are frequently packaged in a great mass of vivid word images which serve to conceal the specific assumptions underlying them; (*b*) A personality theory is by its very nature a general theory of behaviour since it does not focus on certain classes of behavioural events only; (*c*) A personality theory implies a definite formulation about its motivational aspect and the method of understanding its dynamic nature; and (*d*) Personality theories, by and large, prescribe a procedure for the assessment of personality which may be used for professional as well as clinical purposes.

## Measurement (Assessment) of Personality

The measurement or the assessment of one's personality is a difficult task and it is one of the most important areas of evaluation in education. In fact, all the knowledge of psychology helps in understanding of personality of the child and all educational effort is to help in the betterment of the personality makeup of the individual. Different methods are adopted for assessing the personality and all such methods can be broadly categorized under four headings viz., (*i*) Subjective Methods; (*ii*) Objective Methods; (*iii*) Projective Methods; and (iv) Psycho-analytic Methods.

(*i*) ***Subjective Methods*** wherein the information is collected directly from the individual who is being assessed.

(*a*) Observation of behaviour of a person over a long period as one of the techniques of assessing personality traits. The external behaviour of subjects as it happened in controlled and uncontrolled situations can be observed and recorded. It is measurement without instrument. Recording only significant behaviour immediately after observation, and observing at different times, having the purpose of observation in mind proves its usefulness. To evaluate classroom behaviour of students, it is extremely useful.

(*b*) Case Study Method in which the case history has to be re-organized and re-written from infancy up to adulthood. This case history supplies all the large and small facts related to his environment and heredity. This method can be used to study both normal and abnormal people's personalities but it needs very experienced examiners.

(*c*) Interview is a process of communication or interaction in which the interviewee gives the needed information verbally to the interviewer in a face-to-face situation or one-to-one situation. It is a method widely used in the selection of people for government services. It needs very experienced examiners who ask questions which can probe the correct thing and which enable the subject to express himself without any apprehension. It depends as much on the examiner as it does on the subject.

(*d*) Autobiography wherein the child is asked to write his own autobiography and certain personality characteristics can be studied from them.

(*e*) Cumulative Record Card is a useful and permanent record which includes various information about the child.

(*f*) Questionnaires have been used extensively in the investigation of personality. It is the list of selected questions describing certain emotions, traits attitudes or behaviour, the answers to which throw light upon the peculiarities of personality. 'Yes' and 'No' are written in front of these questions. The student either strikes out the wrong answers or indicates the correct one. Questionnaires are used to gain knowledge of traits like self confidence, sociability- introversion or extroversion, tendency to dominate or be dominated etc. They facilitate the study because a number of people can be studied simultaneously. Open form of questionnaire consists of questions to which the subject has to answer freely indicating his opinion. Some limitations are that often the subjects conceal the true facts and give wrong answers, framing of questions is such that the examiner takes them to mean one thing and the subject another and usually the subjects write the answer without an adequate amount of thinking thus, leaving the possibility of mistakes.

(*g*) Introspection is to attend to the working of one's own mind in a systematic way. It is looking within. Individual analyses his own mental process with self observation or looking within self and reports his own thinking, feelings and motives. In the state of anger an individual introspect his own mental feelings and reports it.

*(ii)* ***Objective Methods*** wherein we take the information from others to know the individual. Following are some objective methods of personality measurement that eliminate the subjectivity of interpretation:

(*a*) Rating Scales are used to rate the various personality traits, adjustment, emotions, interests, attitudes and performance on a task. It is done in two ways. One, the subject is asked to answer questions related to traits of personality. The answers which the subject offers or the answers which he selects indicate his personality. Another way of applying the rating method is to place the subject in real situations and then study his behaviour and reactions. For example, in order to judge qualities like skill, honesty, sincerity, labour etc. in a person, he may be given a variety of jobs to perform. But it needs very skillful examiners. It is very difficult to enumerate or evaluate the quality of one subtle quality. Mistakes are often made in this.

(*b*) Check List is employed to collect data about a person. While preparing a checklist to evaluate student's behaviour, a teacher prepares a list of different behaviours from his constant observation of student's participation and behaviour.

(*c*) Controlled Observation under laboratory conditions or under controlled conditions can be used to study certain aspects of personality of an individual.

(*d*) Sociogram in which the sociability of the subject is measured. With the help of this method relationship of the students is judged. It is a very rough and ready manner of getting a working knowledge of the social structure of the class. Each child in a classroom may be asked to mention the name of another child with whom he would like to play or would like to study or would like to go on a picnic or would like to visit during vacation or would like to share his experience and so on. For each of these aspects of life different sociograms can be drawn. First and second choices can be asked for.

(*e*) Personality Inventories wherein an individual's written account of the past behaviour, feelings and wishes can be a good source of information about his personality. Self-ratings can be done through personality inventories and paper and pencil test. Some popular personality inventories are California Tests of Personality, Minnesota Multiphasic Personality Inventory (MMPI), Bell's Adjustment Inventory, Eyeseck's Personality Inventory, Saxena's Personality Inventory, etc.

(*f*) Situation Test in which the subject is placed in some specific situations and the traits of his personality are ascertained. A person is observed in a group situation and conditions. What a person does in a pre-arranged situation and how he does it, are the matters of observation. In some of these tests one way screen is used, so that the observer is not noticeable to the persons in the group.

(*g*) Anecdotal Record is an informal device used by the teacher to record behaviour of students, a significant episode in class or life. It is a written description of a specific incident which the teacher has observed. It furnishes multiple evidences for a good cumulative record maintained for the persons. It stimulates teachers to record the pertinent information to realize about any person.

*(iii)* ***Projective Methods*** wherein the information which cannot be obtained through subjective and objective methods is collected. These projective techniques enable a subject to project his internal feelings, attitudes, needs, values or wishes to an external object. In the projective test situation, the individual responds freely to relatively unstructured yet standard situation to which he is asked to respond. Some of the major projective techniques are:

(*a*) Rorschach's Ink-Blot Test developed by Hermann Rorschach in 1921 uses ten irregular ink-blots standing against a white background. Each inkblot is shown in a fixed number of ways and the testee is asked to report what he sees. In order to establish the meaning of the subject's reaction to the blots, the psychologist analyses the location, deciding factors and the subject. All these things tend to help in the analysis and investigation of the unconscious of the subject. The biggest difficulty in the ink blot test is that description of the subject's reactions becomes quite subjective, which conceals to some extent the correct personality peculiarities of the subject. But maximum efforts are being made to make this test scientific.

(*b*) Thematic Apperception Test (TAT) developed by Morgan and Murray in 1935 requires the subject to look at the picture and to interpret it by telling a story, he is invited to say what led up to the scene in the picture, why such events occurred, and what the consequences will be? Therefore the story expresses his natural desires, emotions, sentiments etc. On the basis of these stories the psychologist analyses the personality of subject and uncovers its traits etc. This test helps in discovery of many mental disorders, enabling subsequently their curing. The personality investigation done by this method is not numerical but qualitative grave possibilities of mistakes. But, still, there is no doubt that an experienced and skillful psychologist can use this method to uncover the traits personality of the subject.

(*c*) Children's Apperception Test (CAT) was developed by Leopold Bellak. The test consists of ten pictures meant for children of the age group 3 to 10. Pictures are shown one after another and reactions or responses are noted and interpreted.

(*d*) Projective Questionnaires wherein the subject is given a series of questions to answer in his own way. Through such questionnaires it is possible to obtain information regarding the subject's emotional life, his values, his attitudes and sentiments.

(*e*) Sentence Completion Tests present a series of incomplete sentences to be completed by the testee in one or more words. Some sample items like, I am worried over ______ , I feel proud when __________ , My hope is _______ , etc.

(*f*) Psychodrama requires the subject to play spontaneously a role assigned to him in a specific situation. It deals with interpersonal relationships and maladjustment problem within the individual.

(*g*) Drawing, Painting and Sculpture wherein artistic productions can also be used as projective techniques. These can be in the form of absolutely unstructured forms like finger paintings or they can be in such form as appears in painting of an individual. The activity of finger painting can be used with adults and children.

(*h*) Machover draw a person test (DAP) wherein Anastani classifies it under expressive methods of projection. This method was devised by Machover in 1949. It attempts to discover personality traits on the basis of children's drawings. It is based on the belief that the child's drawings of human figures represented his own image in relation to his environment.

(*i*) Word association test wherein a list of fifty to hundred stimulated words is read out by the tester; to each word the subject responds with the first word that comes to his mind. He is told not to search about for particularly apt associations. Many of the associations are superficial verbal habits, opposites, rhymes like black – white, father – mother.

(*j*) Story completion test wherein the subject is given one or two descriptions of dramatic events or incomplete plots on the base of which they have to write a story. The story can be got completed orally by small children. Multiple-choice form can also be used in story completion tests.

(*k*) Play technique is very important in the life of the child wherein the child is introduced to a collection of toys which he is permitted to use freely, while the observer notes his activities with respect to the particular items employed, the use made by them, the organization or patterning of toys, attitude towards each toy, vocalizations and general behaviour in the play situation. It provides natural situations relatively free from external inhibiting forces.

*(iv)* ***Psycho-analytic Methods:*** The psycho-analytic method is mostly used in discovering the personality peculiarities, mental complexes and mental ailments of abnormal people. Its min difficulty lies in the need for a skilled and experienced psycho-analyst. Often the psychoanalyst analyses his mind in order to remove the possibility of any prejudice.

(*a*) Word Association Tests wherein the subject is presented a list of words one at a time and is asked to give the first word that comes to his mind. The responses given by the subject and the time taken by him are recorded by the tester for interpretation.

(*b*) Free Association Test in which the subject is allowed to talk for hours together and from it certain traits and behavioural problems are noted.

(*c*) Dream Analysis in which the dream of the subject is analyzed and unconscious behaviour is interpreted. Since 'Dream is the royal road to unconscious', the dream analysis is an effective psychoanalytic method to locate unconscious behaviour of the individual.

The last but not the least and very most important measure of personality is the daily diary. The diary being very personal can contain the record of such events, thoughts and feelings as are of great importance to the student. If properly kept and made available to the counselor, and used by him in confidence, the diary can serve as a useful medium of throwing light upon many aspects of the personality of the individual.

## Functions of Personality

The functions of personality according to Murray and Kluchotm:

> "Personality is the continuity of functional forces and forms manifested through sequences of organized processes in the brain from birth to death." They further observe that "Understanding a personality requires following its development though time, study of the processes of differentiation and integration, knowledge of the personality's endowments."

Some other functions of personality are :

- To allow for the periodic regeneration of energies by sleep.
- To exercise its processes.
- To express its feelings and valuation.
- To reduce successive used tensions.
- To design social programmes foe the attainment of distant goals.
- To reduce conflicts between needs by following schedules, this results in a harmonious way of life.
- To rid itself of irreducible tensions by restricting the number and lowering the levels of goals to be attained.
- To reduce conflicts between personal dispositions and social sanctions, between the vagaries of antisocial impulses and the dictates of the superego by successive compromise formations, the trend of which is towards

a whole-hearted emotional identification with both the conservative and creative forces of society.

## RESEARCH STUDIES

To define intelligence is really difficult task. Psychologists all over the world have made attempts to define intelligence in their best possible language but a satisfactory definition could not be evolved till now. However like the blind men appraising the size of the elephant, many psychologists have defined intelligence in their own way. While the teachers try to measure it nobody seems to know precisely what intelligence is.

The concept of personality like any other is a complex one. Basically the personality of the individual is the main tool with which he is able to carry on inter-action with others. In trying to answer the question 'what is personality' the psychologists have emphasized the various key terms. These are uniqueness, wholeness and integration. Thus most of them hold that personality is the result of the inter-action of heredity and environmental factors and that it is the characteristic whole composed of one's body intellect, temperament and dispositions. It implies the unique way in which one reacts or interacts with the situations in life. As this study intends to find out the intelligence and personality let us look into the findings of the previous studies in the area of intelligence and personality.

### Intelligence and Achievement

Alegaokar (1981) investigated that high achievers in physical achievement had higher I.Q. than low achievers. High achievers in jump and reach, as well as those in long jump and ball throw had higher I.Q. than lower achievers.

Aruna, N.S. (1981) found a significant correlation of 0.44 between intelligence and academic achievement of SC and ST students.

Baruah, Mukul Kumar (1988) found that at level 1 (plus-two stage) students with the highest intelligence level generally go in for the polytechnic course. This was followed by science course, commerce course, arts group and the pharmacy group in that order. At the plus-two stage, students of science stream preferred to go in for the professional stream of study, preferably the engineering and medical courses.

Burwani, Rupa G. (1991) found that intellectual competence had high positive influence upon academic achievement of both science group and commerce group. Academic achievement was positively associated with intellectual competence.

Chatterji, P.S. (1983) found that science students were more intelligent than arts students. Science students achieved significantly higher verbal factor and total intelligence scores than others and they were significantly superior in numerical factor of intelligence in comparison with arts and science students. Scores on intelligence test in science group were significantly higher than others.

Chaudhary, N. (1971) found the correlation coefficient between n-achievement and intelligence scores for the combined samples and for the boys were not significant, whereas the same was significant at 0.01 level for girls. N-achievement and intelligence were significantly positively related was rejected.

Chauhan, S.S. (1984) found that the achievement motivation of students differed significantly at different levels of intelligence, high, middle and low.

Garga, Satish Chandra (1951) found coefficient between memory span and intelligence to be relatively high and are in the range of 0.60 and 0.70.

Gupta, B.D. (1988) found that science teachers were more intelligent than arts teachers.

Jain, S. (1983) found that the high intelligent high achievement motivation group was significantly better in concept formation ability by employing patristic strategy.

Jogi, J.K. (1984) found that intelligence had a significant effect on the achievement.

Kabu (1980) investigated that factor of intelligence was found to have significant influence on mathematical talent at the under-graduate level.

Kumari, Darsahana (1986) found that students with high intellectual commitment were more interested in science than those with low intellectual commitment.

Kumari, Indira (1990) found that children with high intelligence achieved conservation of mass, weight and volume easier than those who were of low intelligence.

Kumari, Indira and Dagaur, B.S. (1992) found that development of mass, weight and volume conservation was positively related to intelligence. Development of seriation and classification abilities appeared to be significantly related to the level of intelligence in children.

Manoranjan, Panda (2005) found a significant difference in academic achievement of students studying in different categories of schools. There is low relationship between academic achievement and intelligence in different categories of schools.

Mehta, P. and others (1967) found that n-achievement has a positive correlation with intelligence.

Pareek, D.L. (1990) found that adolescents studying in private and central schools were more intelligent than in government schools.

Patil, I. (1982) found no significant difference in the n-achievement of superior and average boys.

Ray, Mrinmarji (1988) found that the mean intelligence scores of Santhals were significantly higher than those of Koras.

Saulade, S.D. (1989) found that high intelligent students took less number of trails and committed fewer errors than low intelligent subjects.

Shah, Suhasini (1992) found that the intelligence scores of all the groups showed a significant increase, particularly for items of opposite words, class identification, mathematical reasoning and social reasoning.

Sharma, K. (1981) found no significant difference between science and arts students with respect to verbal ability. A significant difference was found between science and arts students in GIT, numerical and non-verbal activity.

Sharma, K.L. (1978) investigated that achievement showed highest relationship with intelligence.

Sunil Kiran, K.S. (2005) investigated that there is difference in emotional intelligence on academic achievement. Bi.P.C. students have more emotional intelligence than M.P.C. students.

Tripathi, R.C. (1986) investigated that achievement motivation of boys and girls was highly correlated with intelligence and achievement.

Vidhu, M. (1968) investigated that correlation between intelligence and academic performance was positive and highly significant.

Yadav, R.S. (1991) investigated that schooling raised the level of intelligence. Hence, and enriched academic environment, such as use of better methods of teaching, quality of content, guidance, motivation, home assignments, supervision and continuous feedback, etc. may raise the levels of learning and of intelligence.

## Intelligence and Adjustment

Gupta, V.K. (1976) observed that intelligence did not influence significantly the response style and did not bring about any significant difference in extreme response style.

Sharma, K.G. (1972) showed that adjustment was at least partly dependent upon intelligence.

Sharma, M. (1980) showed that intelligence and school satisfaction were highly related. There was a significant difference in intelligence scores of satisfied and dissatisfied students.

Singh, Y. (1978) showed that superior children did not differ from the average children in case of school, health, social and emotional adjustment.

## Intelligence and Age

Ajwani (1979) reported that age had no effect on the problem-solving ability of subjects. The effect of direction of the problem-solving ability was found to be independent of young or old age.

Alegaokar (1981) reported that high achievers in physical achievement had higher I.Q. than low achievers for the students of 13, 14, 15 and 16 years of age. High achievers in jump and reach, as well as those in long jump and ball throw had higher I.Q. than lower achievers of all age groups taken together and separately.

Amin (1982) reported that intelligence was moderately but positively correlated to conservation of length and area. Intelligence was negative and moderately correlated with spatial ego-centrism.

Desai (1971) reported that boys in the first through seventh birth orders did not differ in verbal intelligence. The first born girls had highest verbal I.Q., significantly higher than I.Q. of third born, the fourth and the fifth born. The first born girls excelled the boys in all the birth orders. First born and second born girls did not differ in their I.Q.

Jabbal (1981) reported that age had a significant effect on concept formation.

Kumari, Indira (1990) reported that children of high intelligence seriated and classified objects at an earlier age.

Murthy, Venkatesha (1988) reported that order of birth and intelligence were not related.

## Intelligence and Attitude

Zahir, Saida (1988) reported that mother's negative attitude had an adverse effect on the child's academic performance.

## Intelligence and Creativity

Bharadwaj, R.L. (1978) showed that intelligence was positive with creativity.

Gupta, A.K. (1980) showed that creativity whether verbal or non-verbal was independent of intelligence.

Gupta, Krishna Kumari (1988) showed that creativity had a significant correspondence with intelligence from Grade VI to Grade VIII i.e. from the age of 11 to 13 years, both in urban and rural areas. These were a decline in the relationship between creativity and intelligence at Grade level IX to X i.e. from the age of 14 to 15, both in urban and rural areas.

Komarik (1972) showed no significant relationship between creativity and intelligence.

Muddu, V. (1980) showed that high creative group was found to be negatively correlated with intelligence. Relationship between intelligence and fluency and originality were positive and significant. No significant relationship between high intelligent group and the low creative group and between high creative group and the intelligent group.

Pramod, Ku Prusty (2001) showed that intelligence had significant, moderate and positive relationship with creativity. High intelligence and low int elligent groups do not differ from each other in their creative thinking.

Qureshi, A.N. (1980) showed that intelligence was significant and positively correlated to creativity.

Sen Gupta, M. (1979) showed that high and low creative's differed significantly on intelligence and mechanical reasoning.

Singh, O.P. (1982) showed that the mean intelligence test scores of the science students were significantly higher than that of the arts students.

## Intelligence and Gender

Ajwani (1979) reported that sex had no effect on the problem-solving ability of subjects. The effect of direction of the problem-solving ability was found to be independent of male or female sex.

Bhatttacaryya, Anjana (1989) reported that boys performed better than girls on verbal reasoning test. In abstract reasoning test boys showed superiority over girls.

Dei, S.L. (1991) reported no significant difference between boys and girls on general intelligence.

Gupta, Jyothika and Ram, Sukhjinder (2006) reported no interaction effect of emotional intelligence and sex on any transactional style.

Gupta, K.L. (1977) found a significant difference at 0.01 level in the intelligence of boys and girls, with boys having higher intelligence.

Jit, R. (1985) found significant sex differences in performance on verbal and spatial tasks and moderate sex differences in performance on numerical tasks.

Kar, S.B. (1961) found that in Pass Along Test, school boys were superior to the men and both these groups superior to women. In Block Design Test women were more homogenous than boys. In Porteus Maze Test no significant difference between school boys and the men but both the groups was superior to the women.

Kumar, D. (1981) found no significant difference in verbal and spatial abilities of students of two sexes.

Kumari, Darshana (1986) found a positive relationship of intellectual commitment with interest in science for boys and with interest in humanities for girls. Intelligence and introversion were major contributors towards academic achievement of boys and intelligence and intellectual commitment were major contributors towards academic achievement of girls. No sex differences in intellectual commitment.

Magotra, H.P. (1982) reported that girls scored higher in intelligence test and socio-economic questionnaire than boys.

Panda, S. (1991) reported that girls scored higher than boys on the intellectual ability test which showed progressive decline with increasing age.

Pandey, Asha (2004) reported that boys and girls of the CBSE do not appear to show significant difference in their cognitive competency in so far as geography oriented environmental curriculum is concerned.

Pillai, K.S. (1981) reported that in the high intelligent group, sex differences were found in spatial abilities. In the average intelligent group, sex differences were found in all variables except attitude towards science and formulation. In the low intelligent group, sex differences were found in science aptitude, number series, verbal comprehension and interpretation, interest in science and spatial ability.

Prakash, V. (1986) reported that boys having university position were more intelligent than those having university participation. Similarly boys having inter-university position were more intelligent than those having university participation. Girls belonging to university position, inter-university participation and inter-university position groups possessed higher intelligence than girls having university participation.

Ray, Mrinmarji (1988) reported that there was no significant difference in the intelligence scores of Santhal females and Kora females and Kora males and Kora females. The difference in the intelligence scores of Santhal males and females was significant.

Sahai, S.K. (1985) reported that males were higher on mean intelligence as compared to females.

Selwyn, S. and Ben, Sam W. (2004) reported a significant difference between male and female students in numerical ability and intelligence. Female students were more serious in their work and more imaginative. Science based students had sound exposure to rationalistic thinking.

Singh, K.K. (1985) reported that boys were superior in intelligence to girls.

Self concept had a low positive relationship with attitude towards teaching profession in the sub groups of male students with arts as well as science background, female students with arts background, all arts group students and all male students.

Sunil, Kiran K.S. (2005) investigated that men students have low emotional intelligence than women students.

Tripathi, R.C. (1986) investigated that girls had better average scores in intelligence and boys were better adjusted.

## Intelligence and Home Background

Kumar, Pramod N. (2004) showed no significant difference in performance of juvenile and government school students. Scores of the lower performer of ZPPH School is higher than the lower performer of juvenile school.

Ramiah, L. (1990) showed that parental involvement was relatively low and poor on the educational and intellectual dimensions.

Singh, Y. (1978) showed that superior children did not differ from the average children in case of home adjustment.

Yadav, R.S. (1991) showed that heredity sets the upper limit in the development of intelligence. Intelligence, termed as the ability of the individuals, is contributed to 80 per cent by heredity and 20 per cent by environmental factors.

## Intelligence and Locality

Bhatttacaryya, Anjana (1989) found that urban students performed better than rural students on verbal reasoning test. Rural boys performed better than rural girls. Urban girls showed superiority over rural girls.

Gupta, K.L. (1977) found that rural and urban location was not related to intelligence.

Jabbal (1981) reported that locality had a significant effect on concept formation.

Manoranjan, Panda (2005) found no significant difference in intelligence of students studying in different categories of schools.

Sunil, Kiran K.S. (2005) investigated that there is difference in emotional intelligence on academic achievement of urban and rural students, but not significant. Rural students have more emotional intelligence than urban students. Urban students managed their emotions poorly than rural students.

Tripathi, R.C. (1986) investigated that urban science girls generally secured better scores on their intelligence tests.

## Intelligence and Personality or Personality and Intelligence

Acharya, P. (1991) reported that there was a negative significant correlation between MFFT (Matching Familiar Figure Test) errors and succorance. There was a high negative significant relationship between MFFT errors and RPM (Raven's Progressive Matrices) scores.

Adaval (1973) reported that high level of anxiety, lack of confidence, submissiveness, group dependency and low ego-strength was correlated with conformity behaviour. Conformity was not significantly correlated with intelligence, conservatism and shyness separately.

Agarwal, R. (1985) reported a significant relationship between self-concept and personality characteristics.

Ajwani (1979) reported that the interaction between personality factors and intelligence had no effect on the problem-solving ability of subjects. The effect of direction of the problem-solving ability was found to be independent of facilitatory or inhibitory personality and high or low levels of intelligence.

Arunima (1989) reported that aggressive children scored lower on intelligence than non-aggressive children.

Asthana, Usha (1990) reported that internal warm hearted, emotionally stable and assertive individuals performed better if they worked under intrinsic motivation. Those who were reserved in nature performed better under the condition of external reinforcement-praise. Those who were relaxed and were external in their locus of control did not perform well under any conditions of control. Those who were warm-hearted, assertive, adventurous and tense, performed well irrespective of conditions of control.

Aurora (1980) reported that non-deviants possessed a comparatively better personality. Their self sentiment attainment was good, ego and super-ego were strong. They were radical, submissive and desurgent and were realistic in dealings. In withdrawing deviant's ego, super-ego and self sentiment were anemic. Intelligence remained retarded in adjustive function. Expectation evasion deviants suffered from dryness of emotionality.

Bhagavathy, G.P.K. (1977) reported that there were significant differences in personality variables and intelligence (both verbal and non verbal) between the four deviant and one normal group studies.

Bhatnagar, R.P. (1967) reported that personality and intelligence were found to be significantly correlated. It was found that the need for achievement autonomy, intraception, succorance dominance, nurturance, endurance and aggression correlated positively and the need for deference, affiliation and abasement correlated negatively to the academic achievement of the students.

Bhoj, A.N.T. (1992) reported that introversion/ extraversion scores showed no association with the patterns of cerebral dominance neuroticism.

Chhotray, M. (1991) reported that the humorous and the non-humorous groups of children did not show differential patterns in ascribing seriousness to the 15 coping problems. Children of humorous group did not report the feeling of being insulted when confronted with the problem situation. Emotional reactions were more specific. They possessed coping strategies which involved seeking social support, emotional support and information.

Chinara, B.D. (1992) reported that the clarifying-response strategy was found to be more effective than the self-confrontation strategy for educating adolescents in individual dignity and tolerance.

Chopra, Reeta and Gartia, Radhakanta (2009) reported that the coefficient of correlation between teacher's accountability and occupational stress is negative and significant at 0.01 level. It indicates that teachers who are highly stressed occupationally are less accountable; on the other hand teachers who are less occupationally stressed are more accountable towards their profession.

Dubey (1980) reported that there was a great effect of frustration among the intelligent group.

Dutt, Sunil (1989) reported that high intelligent students scored higher on problem solving ability than low intelligent students. Cognitive style and intelligence were found to contribute significantly to the total variance in problem solving ability.

Godbole, A.Y. (1988) reported that story telling had a positive effect for a wide variety of people irrespective of their intelligence and linguistic skills.

Gupta, Sushma (1991) reported that non-deprived students were more intelligent, more creative and more high achievement learning than deprived students. The deprived students were over protected, depressive, submissive and worried, however they showed a high academic self concept.

Jabbal (1981) could find correlation coefficient between intelligence and mathematical concept formation to be 0.90.

Jailkhani, Neerja (1988) reported that the experimental group gained significantly more I.Q. scores but not the control group.

Jain, Jayanti, R. (1990) reported a positive self concept of adolescent girls and superior cognitive abilities went together significantly. There was a negative relationship between frustration and academic goals.

Jaluria, Reeta (1988) reported that humour in adolescents was more a product than a process of personality, creativity and frustration. Affinity of humour to emotional dryness, ego, self-sentiment, integration, dominance, social boldness showed that it had its own personality.

Jani, Neelima (1990) reported that perception of subjects was not influenced by their security feelings and self-esteem.

Jain, R. (1974) reported that intelligence and introversion were found to be correlated with inter-sensory transfer. Rigidity, intolerance of ambiguity and extroversion were not found to be related to transfer.

Jain, S. (1983) reported that intelligence was found to be a good predictor of nature, form and kind of concept formation ability. High intelligence students scored significantly higher on concept formation than lower ones. Verbal intelligence was found to be the greatest significant interactional effect on concept formation and a positive linear significant relationship between the students scores on test of concept formation and verbal intelligence existed.

Kabu (1980) reported that personality factors were not found to have any consistent pattern in the mathematically gifted of different classes.

Kaur, Satwinderpal (2008) reported that less effective teachers are under a higher level of occupational stress than the highly effective and total group of teachers. Occupational Stress is negatively correlated with the teacher effectiveness, as the stress among teachers increases as their teaching effectiveness decreases.

Kaur, Surinder Jit and Kaur, Harjit's (2006) analysis of the total efforts shows that the efforts which teachers are doing are below average. The teachers are doing the efforts maximum on interpersonal realm and very few on intrapersonal realm and again this percentage is also far below the average.

Kauser (1982) found no significant relationship between curiosity and neuroticism.

Khiangte, Varparhi (1988) found that intelligence, sensitivity, independence, assertiveness and spontaneity were significant correlates of creative thinking abilities observed among secondary school students.

Kumar, J. (1984) found that subjects high on extraversion had greater retention than moderate and low scorers. Extraversion and elaboration of encoding were not independent of each other. Extraversion and retrieval measures did not interact with each other. The three variables, extraversion, elaboration of encoding and retrieval measures were not independent of one another.

Kumari, Sushma (1990) found that in case of juvenile and adult female offenders, no significant differences were observed in case of personality characteristics, intelligence, achievement motivation and adjustment except in case of SES and health adjustment.

Latha (2001) found a positive relationship between Type A behavioural pattern and hardiness. Both are identical in identifying individual's cognitive orientation.

Laxmi, Vibha and Chandel, N.P.S. (2008) found that the non-verbal classroom communication behaviour of pupil teachers is highly positive correlated with teaching effectiveness. There is a significant difference between mean scores of gesture, eye contact, posture, kinesics and paralanguage of highly effective pupil teachers and lowly effective pupil teachers. The non-verbal classroom communication of the pupil teachers was found to be above average. Most of the pupil teachers pay more attention to keeping proper eye contact and using proper paralanguage in classroom teaching. A large number of B.Ed. Trainees are moderately effective.

Madhumathi, C. (1988) found that almost all the convicts had a happy childhood experience, were against violence, with high opinion about police and movies, with high faith in religion and well adjusted. Majority of subjects found to be reserved, assertive, tender minded, imaginative, shrewd, experimenting, self sufficient and tensed. Casual offenders were less intelligent and sober and more expedient whereas habitual offenders were more intelligent and happy go-lucky and conscientious, most of the convicts seemed to be emotionally stable but suspicious.

Manoj, Kumar Dash (2005) found that there exist individual differences with respect to decision making ability.

Misra, K.N. (1991) found that teachers varying in personality and working under different management types used different coping behaviours to reduce their stress and conflicts. Being conscious about duty and patient in problematic situations, tried to adjust to the situation and solve the problem. They were identified as the most frequently adopted behaviours in stressful and conflicting situations.

Murthy, Venkatesha (1988) found that juvenile delinquents and non-delinquents differed significantly in their intelligence level. A majority of non-delinquents were less intelligent as compared to non-delinquents.

Ojha, R.K. (1962) found positive relationship between intellectual stimulation and different aspects of intelligence measured by Vernon's Non-Verbal group test, Vernon's Pattern Drawing test and Vernon's Graded Arithmetic test.

Pal, Yesh (1992) found that the total redundancy co-efficient for personality and intelligence were 2.8 and 13.4 per cent. Personality traits predicted 13 per cent of total variance of intelligence domain. The subjects covered by the students on the relationship between intelligence and personality had been mostly cross-sections of young and old children, adolescents, normal adults, males, neurotic children, children of elementary school, nurses, male medical and psychiatric patients.

Pandey, Sarala and Deb, Rakhi (2008) found that mean value for teaching profession, child-centered practice and teacher were high for married women teachers, whereas for classroom teaching, pupil and educational process, the mean value was high for unmarried women teachers.

Pareek, D.L. (1990) found that there exists no significant relationship between personality traits and level of aspiration among students from different types of schools.

Patel, S. (1983) found that the students from traditional and public schools differed considerably in intelligence.

Patel, S.S. (1982) found a positive relationship between general ability and reading readiness.

Patil, I. (1982) found that the superior and average groups differed significantly in respect of four needs: order, succorance, dominance and endurance. The superior group showed a higher degree of need for order and endurance whereas the average group showed a higher degree of need for succorance and dominance.

Purohit, Surabhi (2008) found that mothers who are supportive, normative and resilient have shown positive relationship with adolescent girl's physical self concept.

Ramesh, R. and Ponnambala, Thiagarajan A. (2005) found that self-concept is above the average i.e. high self-concept in B.Ed. trainees.

Ramganesh, E. and Johnson, N. (2008) found that Emotional Quotient of principals and teacher educators is average. Teacher educators in training colleges and training institutes have the same level of emotional quotient mean. There was no significant gender difference in the level of emotional quotient among teacher educators working in training institutes.

Rao, D.G. (1965) found that differences in aspects of personality were not significantly related to differences in mental abilities.

Rao, N.C.S. (1951) found that performance in concept learning by and large was significantly related to individual differences in intelligence, attitude towards problem solving and ego-strength. There was an interaction between the effects of attitude on strategy and the type of concept task.

Sahai, S.K. (1985) reported that high masculine and high feminine subjects have higher self esteem scores as compared to low masculine and low feminine subjects.

Sambhi, Punam (1989) reported that the personality dimensions of the three groups of students were significantly different. The students of Sri Sathya Sai School were found to be highly intellectual, gregarious, emotional, philosophical, strong and practical and egoistic than those of Missionary schools who were discrete, emotional, intellectual, vivacious, proud and apathetic and rash. Students of Central schools were intellectual, irritable, emotional, rash, bright and timid and mediocre in terms of personality factors.

Samuel, Premela (1988) reported a significant association between moral developmental stage and personality traits. The stages differed with personality traits and some of the social factors like interaction with other students, with teachers and school behaviour. The stages differed with SES, extraversion and intelligence.

Santosh and Kaur, Ravdeep (2009) reported that in the areas of literary, scientific and persuasive interests there seems to be interdependence among SES and vocational interests. On the other hand, in the areas of executive, commercial, constructive, artistic, agricultural, social and household interests there exists no relationship between the two variables, SES and vocational interests.

Selvaraj, Nellaiyappam, Muthumanickam and Suresh Kumar (2005) reported that perception of teachers about allotting more time to teaching slow learners identified by the guide teachers had the lowest frequency with 25 per cent of responses.

Shahin, A. (1971) reported that intelligence and personal-social behaviour developed in an interrelated manner and intelligence and personal-social behaviour were positively related.

Sharma, Archana (1989) reported that both extraversion and neuroticism had positive correlation with psycho-motor performance while intelligence had a lower correlation with it. The correlation between extraversion and reminiscence revealed a significant positive relationship for paired associative figure task only, whereas neuroticism had significant positive correlation with reminiscence for paired associative figure task and paired associative forward tasks.

Sharma, C.S. (1986) reported that the leadership trait was contingent on distinctive on distinctive growth levels of different personality traits.

Sharma, M. (1980) reported that intelligence was an influencing factor in the development of behaviour pattern of the students in all types of schools. Normal adolescents were positively influenced by intelligence, self disclosure and sociometric status.

Sharma, N.K. (1981) reported that extraversion was negatively related to neuroticism and positively related with lie scale.

Shukla, P. (1973) reported that intelligence was highly correlated with space perception.

Singh, E.L. (1979) reported that the differences with respect to simple vs. sophisticated did not turn out to be significant while that for the dependent-self sufficient dimension was significant.

Singh, R.S. (1980) reported a negative correlation between anxiety and ego-strength, anxiety and temperamental traction and no relation between anxiety and intelligence. There was a positive correlation between anxiety and need abasement and nurturance.

Singh, K.K. (1985) reported that personality traits were more or less independent of intelligence. Intelligence linked personality traits of high intelligent subjects showed them to be more scholastic, shrewd and controlled.

Singh, Y. (1978) reported no significant differences in case of teacher's ratings of children for emotional maturity. According to parents, the superior children were more emotionally mature than the average children.

Sridhar, Y.N. and Hamid, Reza Badiei (2007) reported no significant relationship between emotional intelligence and personal efficacy.

Sr. Eve, Justina Remould (2006) reported that intervention programme had a significant impact on the emotional self awareness of student teachers of the experimental group. Treatment had affected the experimental group in their emotional expression. Experimental group members positively responded to the Enneagram educational programme and showed a significant change and improvement in the level of emotional awareness of others.

Sultana, M. (1983) found significant difference between normal and clinical subjects. Normals were more intelligent.

Suresh, K.J. and Joshith, V.P. (2008) found no significant relationship between emotional intelligence and stress, between aided and unaided, between aided and government and unaided and government college student teachers.

Swami, Priyankant M. (1989) reported that the intelligence of normal students was higher than the intelligence of orphan students.

Vasanthi, A. (2008) reported that there is significant difference among the mean scores of decision making style of headmistresses with respect to age, type of institution and problems related to academic activities and with respect to their experience as headmistresses in the area of problems related to co-curricular activities.

Vidhu, M. (1968) reported that introverts were found to take less time than extroverts on Raven's Progressive Matrices.

Zargar, A.H. (1980) reported that the level of expression (high and low) was not related to intelligence.

### Intelligence and Religion

Gupta, Jyothika and Ram, Sukhjinder (2006) showed that intelligence has main effect on Bohemian and Aggressive style.

Sharma, K. (1981) showed significant caste difference in numerical reasoning ability and non-verbal ability.

### Intelligence and Socio-economic Status

Bharadwaj, R.L. (1978) found that intelligence on middle SES was interest promoting. Intelligence at high creativity level promoted vocational interests, the best at the middle level of SES. Intelligence was more vocational interests promoting in low creatives of the middle SES level. Intelligence promoted agricultural interests of high creatives when they belong to middle SES. Intelligence promoted artistic interest in highly ingenious solutions to problems of low originality adolescents of high SES.

Gupta, A.K. (1980) could find a socio-economic status linked factor comprised mainly intelligence and to a lesser extent, non-verbal novelty. Creativity was independent of socio-economic status.

Kumar, D. (1981) found that the intellectual abilities of convent students were more developed than those of higher secondary school students and municipal school students.

Mehta, P. and others (1967) reported that the high SES school boys showed no relationship between n-achievement and intelligence.

Sharma, K. (1981) found no significant SES group differences in verbal, numerical and non-verbal activity.

Sharma, K.L. (1978) could find a weak positive relationship between socio-economic status and intelligence. Sharma, M. (1980) found that intelligence level in moderately high SES and high SES school adolescents were significantly higher than those in the other two categories.

## Intelligence and Values

Vijayalakshmi, G. (2002) revealed that urban teachers scored more mean 132.65 followed by the teachers working in secondary schools mean 129.15 and English medium schools 128.25 in the perception of their values whereas teachers of rural areas 123.11 followed by primary teachers 125.02 and male teachers mean 125.25.

## Personality and Achievement

Abraham, P.A. (1969) reported the influence of the temperamental dimensions of neuroticism and introversion-extraversion on academic achievement showed sex differences. Factor analysis of the personality variables and academic achievement evolved a factor pattern in which three factors could be identified, viz. scholastic aptitude, neuroticism and extraversion-introversion.

Acharya, P. (1991) reported that the reflective group of subjects showed superior performance in comparison to the impulsive performance of personality of individuals.

Ahuja, Malvinder and Tachanut, Yaiuva (2006) reported that low persistence students achieved equal gain means through Multimedia CAI and CGL (Computer Assisted Instructions and Conventional Group Learning). Average persistence students achieved equal gain means through Multimedia CAI and CGL. High persistence students achieved equal gain mean through Multimedia CAI and CGL. Through Multimedia CAI high average and low persistence students were found to be equal in their gain means.

Annie, K. Jacob (2007) reported that the mean of overachievers was found to be higher than the mean of under and normal achievers.

Bharathi, L. (1988) reported that educational qualification and marital status were not found to influence stress among educated working women.

Bhargava, K. (1980) reported that academic competence and schizophrenic personality had negative correlation. There was a negative correlation between neuroticism and academic performance.

Bhatt, Sahdev. (1986) reported that the effect of culture (CT), self-disclosure (SD), obedience-disobedience tendency (ODT) on perception of science teachers (PST) were significant. The interaction effects of CT and SD, CT and ODT and SD and ODT were not significant on PST scores. The low and average students and low and high SD students were significantly different on PST scores. The average and high SD students were not significantly different in PST. Obedient students obtained greater mean PST score than disobedient students.

Burwani, Rupa G. (1991) reported that discrepancies between real and ideal self concept did not affect the academic achievement of commerce group but in the science group real and ideal self concept were positively related. Students who revealed mental ill-health symptoms were poor in academic achievement.

Chandra, Sekhar (2003) reported that there was no high participation in co-curricular activities by the secondary school students. Secondary school students possessed high personality. There was a positive correlation between student's participation in co-curricular activities and their personality development.

Chatterji, P.S. (1983) reported that scores on the extraversion scale in the commerce group were significantly higher than students in science and arts group whereas in agriculture group higher than the scores of arts group.

Chopra, Reeta and Gartia, Radhakanta (2009) found no significant difference in accountability of private and government secondary school teachers.

Dhall, Taruna C. and Salni, Madhu (2008) found that working mother's children receiving high cognitive stimulation have better academic performance as compared to those receiving low cognitive stimulation. No significant difference was observed in academic performance scores of elementary school children belonging to moderate and low cognitive stimulation groups.

Gnanaguru, Selvaraj A. and Kumar, Suresh M. (2008) reported that there is no significant relationship between under achievers achievement score with their home environment and their attitude towards teaching.

Gowri, Prasad (2005) reported no significant difference in stress of government and private school teachers, more experienced and less experienced teachers.

Gupta, Alka (1992) reported that n-achievement, n-affiliation and n-nurturance were positively related.

Gupta, B.D. (1988) reported that effective science teachers had significantly more n-achievement, n-abasement, n-endurance and n-aggression than effective arts teachers. Effective arts teachers had significantly more n-exhibition and n-affiliation than effective science teachers.

Jantli, R.T. (1988) reported that neuroticism and extraversion were significantly and negatively related to academic achievement.

Jayanthi, N.L.N. and Padmanabhan, T. (2008) reported that the test anxiety of the higher secondary students is low.

Joshi, Renuka (1989) reported that the medicine group students scored the lowest on psychoticism and social isolation and the engineering group yielded the highest on these two variables.

Kalpana, Mallela (2003) reported no significant difference between the parental encouragements given to Bi.P.C. and M.P.C. students, boys and girls.

Konwar, L.N. (1989) reported that on school socialization the high groups on achievement orientation, general achievement orientation and overall strength showed higher means of personal achievement scores than the low groups.

Koteswara and Ramachandra, Reddy (2001) reported that all the 14 factors of HSPQ by Cattell's have significant influence on reading achievement of high school students. Students whose personality characteristics were out-going, more intelligent, emotionally stable, excitable, assertive, happy go lucky, super ego strength, venturesome, tense minded, doubting, apprehension, self sufficiency, controlled and tense performed sufficiently better on reading achievement than the students whose personality characteristics were deserved less interested, emotion less, stable, phlegmatic, obedient, jobber, moral, shy, tough-minded, vigorous, placid, group dependent, undisciplined and relaxed.

Madhava, Kale (2007) reported that there was no significant difference between personality of government and private school adolescent boys, private and government urban school adolescent boys, rural school adolescent girls, government and private urban school adolescent girls and boys.

Natarajan and Balan, K. (2003) reported that arts based teachers do not differ significantly in their performance than the science based teachers.

Pareek, D.L. (1990) reported that 45.2 per cent of the adolescents studying in central schools, 44.4 per cent in private schools and 57.6 per cent in government schools possessed average self-concept. Students in government schools were generally practical whereas students in private and central schools were imaginative.

Raina, M.K. and Vats, Arunima (1989) reported that research scholars and doctors differed significantly from administrative officers and lecturers on Type A personality index.

Rajashekar, S. and Raja, Vaiyapuri P. (2008) reported that the teachers handling the subjects of Arts do not differ significantly from the teachers handling the subjects of Science.

Rao, D.G. (1965) found differences in achievement to be significantly related to aspect of personality like neurotic difficulties, morale and sense of responsibility.

Sharma, N.K. (1981) reported that neuroticism is not related with academic achievement.

Saulade, S.D. (1989) reported that extraversion showed a negative relationship with total number of trails, numbers of errors committed and time taken but neuroticism had a positive relationship of these variables.

Sharma, Brajesh Kumar and Patnaik, Sabita Prava (2009) reported that the private schools show highly satisfactory status of organizational health and government and all the schools together show only satisfactory status.

Sharma, S.K. (1986) reported that teaching experience did not affect significantly their class-room behaviour.

Singhaulakh, S.P. (1979) reported that motivation was found to have a significant relationship with better performance and achievement.

Subramonian, G. and Muthaiah, N. (2009) found that graduate and post-graduate students differ in their perception of the quality indicators 'principal as leader', 'teacher and quality of teaching' and 'resources'.

Suresh, K.J. and Joshith, V.P. (2008) found that student teachers of aided and unaided training colleges experience higher stress compared to student teachers of government training colleges.

Uchat, D.A. (1979) reported that students form arts faculty had highest self-concept, science faculty low self-concept and those from the faculty of commerce ranked in the middle.

Rajaram, V. (1995) reported that vigilant style of decision making is associated with positive personality dimensions, though not significant whereas hyper vigilance and defensive avoidance is associated with negative personality dimensions.

Naik, Ramesh H. (2006) reported that teachers with introversion orientation will have greater effect on academic achievement of their students in physical science than teachers with extraversion orientation. There was a significant difference between interaction effects of the introversion/extroversion personality type and effective/ineffective teaching on the academic achievement of their students in physical science.

Saxena, P.C. (1981) studied that a positive self concept was associated with higher academic achievement in mathematics, commerce and arts streams. The under achievers were conspicuously of the opposite type, being aware of their actual difficulties and their need for individual help.

Sharma, Anita (2008) showed that degree college students are more committed in comparison to inter college students. Teachers teaching in inter college and university are equally committed. Teachers teaching in degree college and university are equally committed.

Sharma Brajesh Kumar, Subramanian and Narayana (2006) showed no relationship between self-concept and achievement motivation among boys while a significant positive relationship between self-concept and achievement motivation among girls.

Sinha, D.N. (1966) reported that for the wholesome development of personality it is essential that we ensure success of the individual by feelings of accomplishment and growth.

Srivastava and Saxena (1979) reported that academically successful students were more extravert than academically unsuccessful students.

Vasanthi, A. (2008) reported that there is significant difference among the mean scores of decision making style of headmistresses with respect to educational qualification in the area of problems related to students.

Venkata, Rao (2004) reported that the mean value of high achievers is greater than low achievers. There was a significant difference between the high and low academic achievers with regard to neuroticism. High achievers were more stable than low achievers.

Vidhu, M. (1968) reported that extraversion and academic achievement were negatively associated.

Zahir, Saida (1988) reported that maternal acceptance helped in the development of dominance, self confidence and tendency of extraversion.

## Personality and Adjustment

Acharya, P. (1991) observed that on different personality variables, the reflective and impulsive groups could be different in the case of all but for the two personality variables, succorance and dominance. The correlation between the performance scores on MFFT (Matching Familiar Figure Test) scores and EPPS (Edward Personal Performance Schedule) personality variables revealed an insignificant relationship except for three variables, differentiation, succorance and consistency.

Aggarwal, Vigya (1989) observed a significant correlation among perception of quality of working life and locus of control and employee's job satisfaction. Significant correlation was found between some of the organizational climate variables and perception of quality of working life. Job satisfaction was a predictor of quality of working life.

Bhadury, J. (1989) observed that psychotism, psychopathic deviation, neuroticism, delinquency, anti-social behaviour and jealousy had a positive relationship with each other.

Bharambe, M.D. and Pandit, K.L. (1991) observed the influence of school atmosphere in the pre experimental and the first change observed on attitude towards work, both measured by the paper-pencil test and observation-cum-performance test. A significant interaction between treatment and school atmosphere were found in the second stage of attitude towards work measured by the observation-cum-performance test.

Bhargava, K. (1980) observed a low and negative relationship between schizophrenia and self disclosure.

Chamundeswari, S. and Vasanthi, S. (2009) observed a significant difference in job satisfaction and occupational commitment between teachers in different categories of schools namely state, matriculation and central board schools. The matriculation school teachers have better job satisfaction when compared to the state board school teachers. The central board teachers have better job satisfaction when compared to the state board school teachers and matriculation board teachers. The matriculation school teachers have more occupational commitment when compared to the state board school teachers.

Chatterji, P.S. (1983) observed that commerce and agricultural students obtained significantly higher extraversion scored in comparison to those in the arts and science groups. Students of the agriculture, arts and science groups attained significantly higher neuroticism scores in comparison to those in the commerce group.

Chopra, Reeta and Gartia, Radhakanta (2009) observed that out of 120 secondary school teachers, 24 teachers i.e. 20 per cent teachers are highly stressed occupationally, 65 teachers i.e. 54 per cent are moderately stressed occupationally and the rest 31 teachers i.e. 26 per cent teachers are less stressed occupationally.

Dhillon (1979) observed that participants scored higher on extraversion than non-participants. Participants scored significantly higher on the dimensions of neuroticism than non-participants.

Gaikwad, J.M. (1988) observed that marital adjustment and child rearing practices seemed to be of slight influence in developing outgoing and emotionally stable characteristics in children. Harmonious marital adjustment was seen as remotely associated with the development of placid and relaxed qualities of personality. Emotional instability was more among children coming from families where marital adjustment was poor.

Godbole, A.Y. (1988) observed that the improvement was significant in four problem areas: home adjustment, school adjustment, mental health and general behaviour. Comparison of pre-test and post-test performance of experimental group on adjustment and personality inventory scale showed that there was a significant improvement by the post-test time.

Gupta, B.D. (1988) observed that effective arts teachers were significantly higher than effective science teachers on adjustment. Effective arts and science teachers did not differ with respect to professional adjustment. Effective arts teachers were significantly better adjusted socially, psychologically and physically than effective science teachers.

Hementha, Kumar (2003) observed that girls with average social isolation were found to face more intensity of problems in personal inadequacies, aspirations and life goals, recreation, moral, religious and spiritual aspects, academic achievement, cultural customs and traditions and customs and financial, money, and economic issues than girls with low social isolation. Girls with high social isolation were found to face more intensity of problems than girls with low social isolation and average social isolation.

Johnson, S.J. (1982) observed that sports participants differed from non sports participants in their personality characteristics. Sports participants were more adjusted, free from abnormal tendencies, more sociable (gregarious) and thoughtful (less impulsive) than non-sports participants.

Karunanidhi and Kaliappan (1997) observed that state anxiety, anger-in, occupational stress and certain personality characteristics such as lower ego-strength, pro-tension, group adherence and high self-concept control influenced writer's cramp.

Kumari, Sushma (1990) observed that offenders were maladjusted in all the areas of adjustment.

Lakshmi, Rupa and Ran, Bijay Narayan Sinha (1996) observed that those on high and low on decisiveness, responsibility, masculinity, friendliness, heterosexuality, ego-strength, curiosity and dominance dimensions of personality did not differ significantly in terms of their depression scores. High and low scores on emotional stability groups differ significantly in terms of their depression scores.

Madhava, Kale (2007) observed that the secondary school adolescent girls are extroverts.

Murthy, Venkatesha and Rao, T.R. (1987) observed that the japa practicing and non japa practicing groups did not differ on their personality.

Pareek, A. (1984) observed that environment played an important role in the building of the personality.

Rai, N.K. (1988) observed that sighted children showed poor adjustment on school relationship and leadership than blind children.

Raina, M.K. and Vats Arunima (1989) observed that doctors differed from lecturers, research scholars and administrative officers on variable of involved striving.

Rao, D.G. (1965) observed that academic adjustment significantly related to aspects of personality.

Sharma, Brajesh Kumar and Patnaik, Sabita Prava (2009) observed that the teachers of private schools are highly satisfied whereas the teachers of government schools are only above average in job satisfaction. There is a positive and substantive correlation between organizational health of schools and job satisfaction of teachers.

Sharma, M. (1980) reported that the satisfied and dissatisfied students differed significantly in almost all the personality traits measured through the HSPQ.

Sharma, N.K. (1981) reported that urban youth's achievement motivation was positively related with parental adjustment.

Singh, E.L. (1979) reported that high and low superstitious persons differed significantly on all dimensions except simple vs. sophisticated. Factor of superstitiousness interacted with the locus of control factors in respect of emotion vs. mature, submissive vs. dominance, casual vs. conscientious and conservative vs. experimenting dimension. High superstitious persons displayed poor adjustment in home, health and social areas and a marginal adjustment in emotional and exceptional spheres. An individual's position on the simple sophisticated dimension was determined jointly by the level of superstitiousness.

Swami, Priyankant M. (1989) observed that the self concept of normal students was better than that of orphan students, orphan students being more anxious.

Tiwari, Rajesh Kumar (1997) observed no significant difference between smokers and non-smokers in respect of extraversion. Anxiety, insecurity, neuroticism and poor adjustment lead to the manifestation of smoking habits. Extraversion-introversion dimension is unrelated with smoking. Introverts smoke cigarettes for tranquilizing purposes whereas extraverts smoke for stimulating purposes.

Vijayalakshmi, G. and Lavanya, P. (2006) reported that the management, medium of instruction of the college does not have any effect on stress.

Vijayalakshmi, R. (1991) reported that the family reared and institution reared children were similar in their personality adjustment. The self concept of these children was related to their personality adjustment.

Zahir, Saida (1988) reported that neuroticism was developed by the mother's detachment. Child centeredness made adolescents more sociable and introvert.

## Personality and Age

Agochiya, Devindra Pal (1992) revealed that youth workers scored higher on altruism and lower on psychotism, extraversion and neuroticism.

Bharamble, M.D. (1991) revealed a change in attitude of children in age groups of 8 to 9 years.

Chandresekhar, K. (2006) revealed no significant difference of perception with respect to different age groups.

Chaturvedi, R.D. (1988) revealed that attitude was prone to change with age levels of adolescence, adulthood and senescence and usually it declined after adulthood.

Dixit (1963) revealed that at the age of 5, children indicated fairly good receptivity and responsiveness to the world around, the perception was undifferentiated and was mostly governed by what was obvious. At the age of 7, perception was guided more by facts than by fantasy and emotion. At the age of 8+, children were factual and realistic in manner of responding. At the age of 10+, perception was more influenced by the form of qualities of the blot than by fantasy and emotions and was realistic and factual.

Hussain, M.Q. (1963) revealed that age influenced personality adjustment. On Personality Scales, the tendency of normals was to rate higher than criminals except on age.

Pandey, Sarala and Deb, Rakhi (2008) revealed no significant difference between age and professional attitude for married and unmarried women teachers.

Singh, B.K. (1980) revealed that 5 year old girls were significantly more feminine than 3 and 4 year old girls. 4 and 5 year old boys were significantly more masculine than 3 year old boys.

Uchat, D.A. (1979) revealed that birth order had no relation with self-concept.

Vidhu, M. (1968) revealed that extraversion and neuroticism were negatively related to age (age groups from 15 to 20 and from 20 to 25 years).

## Personality and Attitude

Akthar, S.N. (1970) reported that there was maximum attitude modifiability in subjects who were low on neuroticism, extraversion, authoritarianism and rigidity and high on manifest anxiety. Personality variables influenced the extent of attitude modifiability in persuasive situations. A person whose attitude was highly modifiable was low on neuroticism, extraversion, authoritarianism and rigidity and was highly anxious.

Ansari, Md. F.B. (1974) reported that there was a positive and significant correlation between rigidity and dominance, rigidity and introversion, rigidity and neuroticism, introversion and dominance and self sufficiency and dominance. There was a significant negative correlation between introversion and dominance, introversion and self sufficiency, neuroticism and dominance and neuroticism and self sufficiency.

Bhadury, J. (1989) reported that feedback was effective in helping to improve attitude of students towards their teachers, pro-social orientations and pro-social behaviour. Change in attitude and behaviour contributed to improvement in teacher appreciation. Attitude towards teachers, pro-social value orientation and pre-social value orientation had positive relationship with each other. Attitude towards teachers, pro-social behaviour orientation and pre-social behaviour orientation had a negative relationship with psychotism, psychopathic deviation, neuroticism, delinquency, anti-social behaviour and jealousy.

Bhushan, R. (1985) reported that personality and attitudinal factors were closely related to belief in superstitions. Factors like intolerance of ambiguity, neuroticism, authoritarianism and religiosity were positively related to superstition, while extraversion had no significant relationship with superstition.

Chaturvedi, R.D. (1988) reported that attitude towards social change was associated with empathic outlook in people possessing dominance, radicalism and independence. In association with non-empathetic outlook was noted in people oriented to submissiveness, conservation and subduedness. In conservative people, attitude towards social change was traditionistic throughout the aged period and was non-emphatic up to adulthood with a shift to empathy in senescence.

Chopra, Reeta and Gartia, Radhakanta (2009) observed that out of 120 secondary school teachers, 22 teachers i.e. 18 per cent teachers are highly accountable, 74 teachers i.e. 62 per cent are moderately accountable and the rest 24 teachers i.e. 20 per cent teachers are less accountable towards their job.

Gupta, Alka (1992) reported that most satisfied students were significantly higher on n-achievement, n-nurturance and n-endurance while least satisfied students were higher on n-exhibition, n-dominance and n-aggression.

Khan, Saheel Md. and Srivastava, Bina (2008) reported that teachers with poor mental health are prone to more burnout than the average and good mental health groups.

Mishra, Brundaban and Patel, Bananli (1990) reported that improvement in direct teacher talk and teacher's response ration brought about improvement in students liking.

Mishra, G. Santwana (2007) reported that the attitude of trainee teachers is not influenced by the trainee teacher gender, qualification and geographic location.

Pandey, Sarala and Deb, Rakhi (2008) reported that as for professional attitude, mean value was high for unmarried teachers but there was no significant difference between married and unmarried teachers.

Pareek, D.L. (1990) reported that adolescents in central and government schools preferred science subjects while adolescents in private schools preferred arts stream.

Pradhan, Renuka (1990) reported that personality and inter-personal attraction were correlated with each other. Attraction was based on similarity of attitudes and attitude and personality were related to each other.

Raghu, A. and Mahender, Reddy S. (2008) reported no significant difference between male and female student teachers, arts and science student teachers, private and government colleges, graduate and post-graduate student teachers, between private male and private female student teachers, between government female and government male student teachers, government graduate and post-graduate student teachers, private government and post graduate student teachers and between private female and government female student teachers with regard to their attitude towards micro teaching. There is a significant difference between government science student teachers and government arts student teachers, between private science and arts student teachers, between private graduate and government post graduate student teachers with respect to their attitude towards micro teaching.

Sharma, Mala and Sharma, Suman (2009) reported that there is no significant difference in the attitude of male and female secondary teachers and those having experience below 10 years and 10 to 20 years towards project method of teaching Science. There is a significant difference in the attitude of public school and government aided school, secondary classes and senior secondary classes science teachers.

## Personality and Creativity

Annie, K. Jacob (2007) found that higher mean value of overachievers indicates that they possess more verbal creative abilities compared to under and normal achievers. No significant difference among three groups i.e. the low, normal and high achievers do not vary in respect of mean non verbal creativity scores. Self- concept is significantly correlated to creativity. A positive self-concept enhances the creativity among students who are overachievers.

Bali (1981) found that Poets possessed factors like emotional sensitivity and creative mood and social will, Painters profile consists of factors like emotional sensitivity and creative mood and Scientists like ego-ideal, emotional introversion and social will and Musicians like ego-ideal and social will.

Cacha (1976) attempted to determine whether different levels of figural creativity as measured by Torrance Tests were related to personality test as measured by 16 PF test and observed that figural creativity was related to happy-go-lucky, socially bold, relaxed and extroverted behaviour. A multiple correlation of 0.38 was obtained between creativity and some personality factors like shy *vs.* venturesome, sober *vs.* enthusiastic, relaxed vs. tense and phlegmatic *vs.* excitable.

Dagaur, B.S. (1988) studied that anxiety affected both introverts and extraverts in creative thinking.

Discippio (1971) studied divergent thinking a complex function of interacting dimensions of extroversion-introversion and neuroticism-stability. After controlling verbal intelligence, divergent thinking was sound to be a complex function of extroversion-introversion and neuroticism-stability as measured by Eysenck Personality Inventory. Stable extroverts were significantly more fluent than stable introverts but neurotic introverts and extroverts attained fluency scores approximating the mean of the extreme stable counter parts.

Drevdahl, J.E. (1956) found the creative group to be more interested in scientific investigation, relatively unconcerned with other people, authority, rules, regulations, restrictions and are usually self oriented, without showing much concern to such things as social and sexual relationship and public and professional criticism. He failed to observe any significant difference between the high and the low creatives on expedient-conscientious scores of personality.

Dutt, Bountra and Sabhrawal (1973) found insignificant positive correlation between extroversion and creativity and further observed that high and low creatives could not be significantly differentiated on the extroversion scores.

Fernandez and Venkataraman (2002) found that students belonging to government and private schools are equal in their creative characteristics and ego scales. There was no significant correlation between creative characteristics and ego states, adult ego and child ego.

Halpin, Payne and Elliott (1974) observed that creative scores were highest for students reading social science, art and science groups but lowest for students reading music and foreign language groups.

Jhag (1979) found that creative boys were adventurous while creative girls were shy, timid, restrained and sensitive to threat.

Komarik (1972) studied the relations between creativity and other measures of personality namely intelligence and Eysenck's Orthogonal factors. A significant positive correlation was found between creativity and neuroticism, while no significant relationship was found between creativity and extroversion.

Kubie (1958) held that high creatives need not necessarily be more neurotic than others.

Kurtzman (1967) observed that creative students tend to be more adventurous, extroverted and self confident. They also have a less favourable attitude towards schools. In terms of peer's acceptance, sex appeared to be an important factor. Higher creative boys received greater acceptance while higher creative girls are less accepted by their classmates. He found that the creative individuals tend to be significantly more extroverted.

Muddu, V. (1980) observed that personality characteristics of high creative group totally differed from those of low creative group.

Pal, Yesh (1992) observed that personality factors played vital roles in promoting convergent thinking abilities.

Paramesh (1972) observed that the high creative individuals were neither significantly more nor less introverted than the low creative individuals.

Patel (1976) studied personality syndromes of people who are high on five creativity dimensions, using Torrance Test of Creative Thinking and a Biographical Inventory form along with the 16 PF test and found that those with a high profile on all creativity variables were venturesome, placid, self confident and emotionally stable, while those low on all creative variables were shy.

Payne, Helpin, Ellett and Dale (1975) studied personality correlates of creativeness in two groups: academically and artistically gifted youths and obtained multiple correlations between sub classes of the 16 Personality Factors and Torrance and Khatana's What kind of person are you? Inventory—a measure of creative personality characteristics.

Phillips (1973) found that the high and the low creative subjects differed significantly in terms of some personality factors and the way in which they perceived themselves. It was also found that within each group significant relationships were found between personality profiles and self perceptions. He found a significant negative correlation but the high and the low creative groups could not be differentiated significantly on social extroversion scores.

Sinha and Sharma (1978) failed to observe significant difference between the high and the low creatives on emotional adjustment.

Srivastava, B. (1982) found a positive relationship between the scores on creativity and the scores of different personality factors.

Zargar, A.H. (1980) found that the high and the low neurotic groups did not show any significant difference in creativity.

## Personality and Gender

Agarwal, Richa (1990) reported that goal setting behaviour was a significant determinant of anagram task learning of female students. The success of female adolescents on anagram task learning was significantly influenced by risk taking behaviour.

Arunima (1989) reported that aggression was found to be more in boys than in girls.

Babu, Sameer M. (2009) reported that boys have more self experience than girls. There is significant negative relationship between self experience for the whole sample boys students of parents working abroad and students of parents working in Kerala. There is a negative relationship between the experimental variables in the case of girls.

Bharambe, M.D. and Pandit, K.L. (1991) reported that significant interactions between school atmosphere and sex and treatment and school atmosphere were observed on the first and second change of attitudes towards cleanliness measured by observation-cum-performance test.

Bharamble, M.D. (1991) reported that sex was irrelevant to attitudinal change.

Bharathi, L. (1988) reported that working women who experience a high degree of role conflict would tend to experience a greater degree of stress than other groups. Women having a low degree of Type B personality factors had more stress than the high group in all its dimensions.

Bhoj, A.N.T. (1992) found no significant sex differences on introversion/extraversion dimension of personality.

Chandra, Sekhar (2003) found no significant difference in the participation of co-curricular activities by secondary school boys and girls.

Chandresekhar, K. (2006) found a significant difference with respect to perception in men and women. Women student teachers had higher mean score than men.

Dagaur, B.S. (1988) found that at higher and average levels of neuroticism, there was no significant difference in mean originality scores of males and females. At lower levels of neuroticism, female extraverts showed more flexible and fluent behaviour than introverts.

George, M. (1969) found that in temperament, men were more ascendant, sociable and masculine than women. Women in humanities group had more restrain than men and were emotionally more stable, objective and friendly.

Gowri, Prasad (2005) found no significant difference in stress of men and women school teachers.

Gupta, Alka (1992) reported that the needs for dominance, abasement and aggression were negatively related with academic satisfaction in male graduate students. N-exhibition, n-autonomy, n-succorance and n-endurance were not related with the academic satisfaction of male graduate students. N-achievement, n-nurturance and n-endurance were positively related while n-aggression was negatively related with the academic satisfaction of female graduate students. Male students were higher on n-exhibition, n-autonomy and n-dominance while female students were significantly higher on n-affiliation.

Gupta, K.L. (1977) found that on the endomorphy-viscertonical classification the girls scored significantly higher than boys exhibiting higher endomorphism. Boys were more endomorphic than girls.

Jain, Jayanti, R. (1990) found that girls having high self concept tended to select high academic which were positively associated with each other.

Jani, Neelima (1990) found that male subjects perceived females more favorably as compared to males perceiving males. Female subjects gave more favorable perceptions of male persons as compared to females perceiving females.

Jayanthi, N.L.N. and Padmanabhan, T. (2008) found that male and female students differ significantly in their test anxiety.

Jhag (1979) found that male and female subjects has more or less similar personality styles in respect of the reserved versus outgoing trait.

Joshi, Renuka (1989) found that females were higher on fluency, originality, extraversion and neuroticism than males.

Karuna, Sharma and Sadhana, Mahajan (2001) found that extrovert females experienced significantly more stress in their perception of role erosion, role isolation and role ambiguity whereas in males more stress was felt on role stagnation. Introvert females were more stressed on all types of role stress except role stagnation and personal inadequacy as compared to males. Neurotic females had significant higher stress in their perception of inter role distinction, role overload, role isolation and role ambiguity. Neurotic females experienced more stress on all types of role stress except role stagnation.

Stable males experienced more stress on inter role distinction, role stagnation, personal inadequacy and resource adequacy whereas females experienced more stress on inter role distinction and role erosion.

Kaur, Satwinderpal (2008) found that female secondary school teachers are significantly under more occupational stress than their male counterparts.

Khatoon, J. (1988) found that male students were more phlegmatic, adventurous, tough-minded and placid as compared to female students who were more excitable, shy, tender minded and apprehensive by nature. Interaction between achievement and sex significantly affected personality factors C, $Q_2$ and $Q_4$. Interaction of achievement, sex and locality did not have any significant effect on any personality factors.

Kumar, Anil P.M. and Ayishabhi T.C. (2008) found that boys are not significantly different from girls as far as the awareness of values in the content of secondary school English curriculum is concerned.

Kumari, Shiv (1990) found that under graduate girls were in general more modern than undergraduate boys and they were different in the aspects of modernity. As the level of aspiration rose under graduate boys and undergraduate girls showed a decline in modernity. As self-concept increased, under graduate boys and girls showed significant increase in modernity.

Kumari, Sushma (1991) found that males exhibited extrovert tendencies.

Poulose, P.J. (1988) found that introversion, extraversion, self-concept the interaction of these variables and the sex had no significant effect on process outcome.

Prakash, V. (1986) found that boys of university position group were better on factor M than boys from university position, university participation and inter-university participation groups. Girls having university position and inter-university position and inter-university participation possessed significantly higher personality factor E than girls having university participation.

Purohit, Surabhi (2008) found that mothers with supportive, confronting and innovative style have shown positive relationship and mothers with prescriptive style have shown negative relationship with the social self concept of adolescent girls. Father's supportive and normative styles have shown significant positive relationship with the social self concept of girls, task obsessive style has shown significant negative correlation with the social self concept.

Krishna, K.P. (1973) found that male and female students differed significantly in risk-taking, neuroticism, extraversion, security-insecurity, home adjustment and responsibility dimensions of personality.

Madhava, Kale (2007) found no significant difference between the personality of adolescent boys and girls.

Magotra, H.P. (1982) found that the mental life of boys was dominated by the feelings of depression and neurotic behaviour.

Naik, Ramesh H. (2006) found no significant difference between the interaction effects of male teacher's introversion/ extroversion personality type and favourable/unfavourable attitude towards profession on the academic achievement of their students.

Rajashekar S. and Raja Vaiyapuri, P. (2008) found that the male teachers do not differ significantly from the female teachers.

Sahai, S.K. (1985) found that females were higher on external control as compared to males.

Sharma Brajesh Kumar, Subramanian and Narayana (2006) found that boys and girls show a significant relationship between self-concept and achievement in mathematics.

Sharma, C.S. (1986) found no differences in personality traits of leaders with regard to sex. A leader whether male or female had similar personality by traits.

Sharma, K.L. (1978) found that boys were superior to girls in self concept.

Sharma, N.K. (1981) found that tribal males were highest and urban males lowest on the lie scale.

Sharma, S.K. (1986) found that student's perceptions regarding female teacher's classroom behaviour were better than their perceptions regarding the classroom behaviour of male teachers.

Singh, B.K. (1980) found that personality had a significant effect upon the development of sex-role preference in children.

Singh Tirath and Kaur, Parminder (2008) found that there was significant effect of gender on self confidence when pre self confidence was taken as a covariate.

Srinivas, Kumar (2002) found that irrespective of sex differences, the popular teachers are good teachers who possess certain temperamental traits like reflective, painful, active and responsible characteristics.

Srivastava, P. (1981) found the conservative girls to be more sober, more lax, more tough-minded and less individualistic.

Subhalakshmi, Nandi (2002) found that the proportion of teachers with high and low scores in organizational stress do not bear any gender influence. No significant difference between male and female secondary school teachers with respect to their perception of organizational stress. The distinction differs of perception of high stressed and low stressed group of teachers regarding their work environment.

Subramonian, G. and Muthaiah, N. (2009) found no difference of perception between the male and female students in terms of quality indicators 'principal as leader', 'teacher and quality of teaching' and 'resources'.

Suresh, K.J. and Joshith, V.P. (2008) found that females have higher stress compared to males.

Swami Priyankant, M. (1989) found that sex had no effect in the difference in the self concept of orphan and normal students.

Tripathi, R.C. (1986) found that boys and girls had poor level of aspiration.

Uchat, D.A. (1979) found sex to be related to self-concept. Female students possessed higher self-concept than male students.

Usha, P. and Sasi, Kumar (2007) found no significant relationship between teachers self concept and job satisfaction for male and female teachers.

Venkata, Rao (2004) found no difference of extrovertism and introvertism between boys and girls of high and low achievers.

Verma, B.P. (1990) found that male adolescent learners showed significant higher mean risk taking than female adolescent learners. Male adolescent learners possessed significantly higher self confidence than female adolescents. Female adolescent learners had significantly more anxiety than male adolescent learners.

Vidhu, M. (1968) found that girls scored higher on neuroticism than boys.

Vijayalakshmi, G. and Lavanya P. (2006) found that male students felt more stress than female students.

## Personality and Home Background

Aggarwal, Vigya (1989) found no significant correlation between the background variable and perception of quality of working life.

Arunima (1989) found that aggression in children was not related to aggression in parents. More aggression children were found in the families where parents had low education and income and were engaged in blue-collar jobs. Parents played an important role in making the child aggressive. Aggressive children belong to parents who not only associate positive meanings with physical punishment, but also use it as a mode of child-rearing. Large size of the family was found to be more conducive to making the children aggressive. The younger parents had more aggressive children in comparison to the older parents. Un-congenital childhood and aggressive spousal relations were not found to be associated with aggressive parents.

Babu, Sameer M. (2009) found that there is average self experience in building among students of ninth grade whose parents are working abroad and students of parents working in Kerala. Parental occupation plays a little role on self experience scores.

Baruah, Mukul Kumar (1988) found that difference in family background was not related to the choice of course of study.

Chandresekhar, K. (2006) found that children of housewives evidence more positive perception than other groups.

Fernandez and Venkataraman (2002) found that parent ego had significant correlation with adult ego and child ego.

Hussain, M.Q. (1963) found that home influenced personality adjustment.

Jain, Neera (1989) found that high parental support high school- high control subjected to the development of self-esteem. The interaction of family structure with parental behaviour and that of sex with parental behaviour were found significant. The subjects of joint family were higher on socio-economic power as compared to nuclear family.

Johi, J.K. (1984) found that ego identity was positively and significantly related to the perception of the adolescents of their school and home environment.

Kalpana, Mallela (2003) found that children are given utmost parental encouragement in their academic aspects. There was a significant difference between parental encouragement given to private residential college students and private non-residential college students. Private non-residential college students received more parental encouragement than private residential college students.

Kumar, R.B. (1954) reported that parents had great responsibility in developing a sane successful personality of their children.

Kumari, Sushma (1991) reported that students from a non-deprived home environment were found to be extrovert.

Pal, Anitha (1988) reported that mothers of children with high cooperation were more development-oriented.

Ramiah, L. (1990) reported that there was a significant relationship between parental involvement and self-concept of the students, the more parental involvement the better the self-concept.

Singh, B.K. (1980) reported that upper caste boys and girls were more conscious of their appropriate sex role than lower caste. Personality of parents did not influence the sex role preferences of their children.

Uchat, D.A. (1979) reported that students from advanced class had higher perception of themselves, themselves as students.

Vijayalakshmi, G. and Lavanya, P. (2006) reported that the students having highly educated fathers are feeling more stress.

Vijayalakshmi, R. (1991) reported that family reared and institution reared children were similar in their self concept.

## Personality and Locality

Bhatt, Sahdev (1986) found that Indian students had better perception of science teachers than Nepalese students. But the low self-disclosure (SD) Indian low self-disclosure Nepalese, average SD Indian and average SD Nepalese and high SD Indian and high SD Nepalese were not significantly different on perception of science teacher's scores.

Chandra, Sekhar (2003) found no significant difference in the participation of co-curricular activities by the urban and rural students and government and private school students.

Dalu, Pratibha (1992) found that between rural male and female students the difference was statistically significant for $Q_1$, A, $Q_4$ and in theoretical, aesthetic and religious values.

Gowri, Prasad (2005) reported no significant difference in stress of urban and rural teachers.

Gupta, K.L. (1977) found that urban girls were more endomorphic than the rural girls. The rural girls were more ectomorphic than urban girls.

Hussain, M.Q. (1963) found that locality influenced personality adjustment. On Personality Scales, the tendency of normals was to rate higher than criminals except on locality.

Jayanthi, N.L.N. and Padmanabhan, T. (2008) found that students studying in rural schools have more test anxiety than the students studying in urban schools.

Khatoon, J. (1988) found that rural students achieved higher mean values on factors E and $Q_2$ than urban students. Achievement locality interaction did not affect the personality traits significantly. Rural students tended to be more assertive and self sufficient whereas urban students were obedient and group dependent.

Kumari, Sushma (1990) found that urban and rural juvenile delinquents and adult rural and urban offenders total adjustment was significantly correlated with social and emotional adjustment which were significantly related with each other.

Madhava, Kale (2007) found no significant difference between the personality of rural and urban school adolescent boys and girls.

Poulose, P.J. (1988) found that introversion, extraversion, self-concept the interaction of these variables and the residence had no significant effect on process outcome.

Rajashekar, S. and Raja, Vaiyapuri P. (2008) found that the teachers working in the urban schools do not differ significantly from the teachers working in the rural schools.

Sharma, C.S. (1986) found no differences in personality traits of leaders with regard to locality. There is no significant difference in personality traits of leaders belonging to rural and urban areas.

Sharma, N.K. (1981) found that area emerged as a significant correlate of Lie-Scale (social desirability) with means favouring tribal youth followed by urban and rural youth. Urban males were higher on extraversion than tribal females. Rural youth's extraversion and neuroticism were positively correlated with achievement motivation and adjustment whereas urban youth's extraversion was negatively related to neuroticism.

Srivastava, R.K. (1988) found that urban and rural boys did not differ significantly on personality needs except n-change. On the personality needs of heterosexuality, aggression, abasement, order, endurance and nurturance, female pupils of rural and urban locality differed significantly. The boys and girls of rural areas differed significantly on personality needs for order, exhibition, heterosexuality and endurance.

Subramonian, G. and Muthaiah, N. (2009) found that rural and urban students differ in their perception of the quality indicators 'principal as leader', 'teacher and quality of teaching' and 'resources'.

Usha, P. and Sasi, Kumar (2007) found no significant relationship between teachers self concept and job satisfaction for rural and urban teachers and government and aided school teachers.

Venkata, Rao (2004) found no significant difference between rural and urban achievers on extrovert and introvert.

Vijayalakshmi, G. and Lavanya, P. (2006) found that the locality of the college does not have any effect on stress.

## Personality and Religion

Arunima (1989) found that the aggressive behaviour pattern was not confined to lower castes but transferred the boundaries of castes and class.

Dalu, Pratibha (1992) found that rural male and urban male students did not differ in personality traits and values, these groups differed significantly in religious information, orthodoxy and hostility. Between rural male and rural female students the difference was significantly in factor A, aesthetic values, religious information and religious tranquility.

Hussain, M.Q. (1963) found that religion influenced personality adjustment.

Jayanthi, N.L.N. and Padmanabhan, T. (2008) found that students who belong to SC have more test anxiety than those who belong to BC and students who belong to BC have more test anxiety than those who belong to MBC.

Konwar, L.N. (1989) reported that there was no significant difference in the levels of personal achievement motivation of tribals and non-tribals.

Leela, A.V.S. (1988) found that the difference in mean scores of the high religious group on personality factors of O, $Q_1$, $Q_2$ and $Q_4$ were significantly higher than those for the low group. Personality profiles of high and low religious groups were not similar. High and low religiosity was significantly associated with sex, girls being higher than boys.

Singh, Tirath and Kaur, Parminder (2008) reported no significant effect of religion, interaction between meditation and religion on self confidence when pre self confidence was taken as covariate.

Swami, Priyankant M. (1989) found that self concept of orphan Muslim students and normal students were similar.

## Personality and Socio-economic Status (SES)

Asthana, Anju (1989) reported that SES was not found to contribute to social maturity at any of the five grade levels.

Bharamble, M.D. (1991) reported that school environment and SES were the most important factors in emergence of attitude as well as in bringing attitudinal change.

Bharathi, L. (1988) reported that income was not found to influence stress among educated working women.

Hussain, M.Q. (1963) reported that income influenced personality adjustment.

Jain, Neera (1989) reported that subjects of joint family were higher on socio economic power as compared to nuclear family.

Kumari, Shiv (1990) reported that under graduate boys and under graduate girls belonging to the high SES were significantly more modern than their lower SES group.

Kumari, Sushma (1991) reported that students of high SES showed a high temperament.

Mehta, P. and others (1967) reported that the high SES school boys showed no relationship between n-achievement and performance.

Santosh and Kaur, Ravdeep (2009) reported that there is no significant difference between high and low SES students on executive, commercial, artistic, agricultural, persuasive, social and household areas. On the other hand, there is significant difference between them in the area of literary, scientific, agricultural and persuasive interests.

Sharma, R.K. (1978) reported that behaviour pattern of adolescents in low socio-economic status schools was significantly better than that of adolescents in high socio-economic status schools. Schools SES did not significantly influence the sociometric status of the adolescents. Normal adolescents were negatively influenced by the SES of the family.

## Personality and Values

Agochiya, Devindra Pal (1992) revealed that youth workers were lower on theoretical, economic and aesthetic values, whereas they were higher on social, political and religious values in comparison with other adults. Country-wise comparisons showed significant differences in altruism, extraversion, neuroticism, social desirability, economic values and aesthetic, social, political and religious values but not in psychotism. No significant difference emerged on all the six values and other variables between government and non-government groups and between two sexes.

Chinara, B.D. (1992) revealed that the democratic value preference patterns for various combinations of groups were found curvilinear, which resembled M, N and U in shape under the self-confrontation strategy.

Dalu, Pratibha (1992) revealed that urban male and female students differed significantly in $Q_1$, theoretical, religious and aesthetic values, orthodoxy and hostility. Rural male and urban male students did not differ in personality traits and values, these groups differed significantly in religious information, orthodoxy and hostility.

Kumar Anil, P.M. and Ayishabhi T.C. (2008) revealed that the secondary school English students awareness of values in the content is 36 per cent.

Sandhu, Sadhana (1990) revealed that an interrelationship between Triguna person's inventory and psychoticism, extraversion and neuroticism emerged with sattva and extraversion being negatively related suggesting a positive relationship between sattva and introversion. Sattva was negatively correlated with neuroticism and tamas was positively correlated with psychoticism.

Vijayalakshmi, G. (2002) revealed that the rural and urban teachers differed significantly in their opinion with regard to their values to be developed among school children.

Walberg and Welch (1967) observed that high creative physics teachers scored high on theoretical and aesthetic value but lower on economic and political values.

## Intelligence-Personality and Achievement

Anagha, Lavalekar (2001) found that a purposefully planned and methodically implemented training programme can facilitate the development of awareness of social problems in intellectually superior as well as average students. Superior children are significantly better than the average children in the cognitive aspect of social awareness. They are better in giving motivational responses but no significant difference is found in the average and the superior with respect to urge for action.

Arockiadoss, S. and Karumathur (2006) found average level of learning effectiveness. Science students are more effective in learning than the arts students.

Asthana, Anju (1989) found academic achievement to be related to social maturity in Grades I, II and V only. Intelligence was found to contribute to social maturity in Grades I and IV only.

Bansibihari, Pandit and Lata, Surwade (2006) found that teaching of emotional mature teachers is more effective than those of emotional immature teachers whose teaching is found to be of average grade.

Bansibihari, Pandit (2004) found that the level of emotional intelligence of secondary teachers is low and extremely low, while to be successful in teaching profession and to have job satisfaction one needs a high emotional quotient level in the range of 250 to 274.

Baruah, Mukul Kumar (1988) found that professional groups had intense subjective and inner mental life while non-professional students were guided by subjective realities. Professional students were tough-minded, shrewd and confident while non-professional students were found to be sentimental, depressed, moody and emotionally sensitive.

Batania, Kulwanth Singh (2007) found that orientation programmes help in inculcating confidence, courage and commitment towards their profession amongst the teachers. They are not a mere condition for promotional development but provide an opportunity for self introspection and interaction.

Behera, Laxidhar (2004) found that academic careers of science background student teachers are generally strong as compared to their arts student teachers. IASE's are fully equipped with learning aids, competent and experienced teacher educators and proper library and research facilities than CTE's.

Burwani, Rupa G. (1991) found that students who perceived themselves to be highly competent were relatively free from mental ill-health symptoms.

Darsana, M. (2007) found a significant relationship between emotional intelligence and certain achievement facilitating variables like boys, urban, rural and government institutions, emotional intelligence and self-concept, EI and achievement motivation for boys, urban, rural and private institutions and EI and examination anxiety.

Dhall, Taruna C. and Salni, Madhu (2008) found that children of working mothers having similar intelligence, receiving high cognitive stimulation exhibited higher academic performance as compared to those receiving low cognitive stimulation. Children of non working mothers having similar intelligence, receiving high cognitive stimulation were found to exhibit higher academic performance as compare to those receiving low cognitive stimulation.

Fatima, Shaik (2005) found low reasoning ability in secondary school students. Private English central syllabus students had high reasoning ability than government Telugu state syllabus students.

George, M. (1969) found that among science students, men were more thoughtful while women were found better in personal relations.

Gnanaguru Selvaraj, A. and Kumar Suresh, M. (2008) found that the underachievers have average level of intelligence score, low level achievement score, satisfactory home environment and unfavourable attitude towards teaching.

Godbole, A.Y. (1988) found that the improvement in positive thinking was independent of the improvement in language achievement test or reading listening and comprehension test.

Gupta, B.D. (1988) found that science and arts teachers did not differ significantly with respect to adjustment and academic and general environment of the institution.

Jhag (1979) found no significant difference in the achievement of high creative and high intelligent groups.

John, Louis Manoharan and Christie, Doss (2007) found that the level of emotional maturity of P.G. students is low. They were moderately sound in their personality integration and independence. There was a positive relationship between the group chosen for the study and level of emotional maturity. Science students have greater emotional maturity. Students of 2nd year were more mature than those of the first year.

Joshi, Renuka (1989) found that engineering students were significantly high on fluency and originality followed by the medicine, management and law groups. Extraversion, neuroticism and powerlessness were the highest in engineering group followed by the law, medicine and management groups.

Jyothi, Prathibha A. (2003) found that independent problem solving ability was of average level in secondary school students and no high independent problem solving ability in mathematics secondary school students.

Kumari, Sushma (1990) found that delinquents had low intelligence and achievement motivation.

Laxmidhar, Behera and Sushant, Kumar (2004) found no significant difference in the performance of women student teachers reading in women institutions and co-educational institutions. Science teachers were more superior to arts teachers and superiority of IASE student teachers over the CTE (Colleges of Teacher Education).

Malhotra, D.K. (1982) found that on the easier problems neurotic extroverts gave the best performance and on difficult and complex tasks stable introverts performed the best.

Manoj, Kumar Dash (2005) found that the predominant decision making style of all teacher educator groups was vigilance.

Mishra, G. Santwana (2007) found a negative correlation between attitudes of trainee teachers towards teaching profession with academic score.

Nabi, Ahmed and Abdul, Rahman (2003) found that there would be a significant relationship between criterion variable academic achievement and the predictive variable intelligence.

Narula, K.S. (1979) reported that intelligence was not found to have relationship with n-achievement, affiliation need, endurance and succorance. N-achievement as measured by TAT pictures of Mehta differed significantly between the subjects of high and average intelligents.

Pandey, Sarala and Deb, Rakhi (2008) found no significant difference between teaching experience and professional attitude, educational qualification and professional attitude for married as well as unmarried women teachers.

Patil, Ajaykumar Bhimrao (2006) found no significant difference in emotional intelligence of student teachers of arts and science faculty. There was a significant relationship between emotional intelligence and academic achievement of student teachers.

Ramganesh, E. (2006) found no significant difference in emotional maturity of students having graduate and post-graduate levels of education.

Ramesh, Mandalapu (2005) found that the level of mathematical problem solving ability was high in 9th class students.

Ramesh R. and Ponnambala Thiagarajan A. (2005) found that higher the qualification, higher was the self concept among the B.Ed. trainees. No significant difference in self concept of the respondents in terms of their optional studies.

Saulade, S.D. (1989) found that emotionally stable extraverts took less time to learn the verbal maze than emotionally unstable introverts.

Sharma, Brajesh Kumar and Patnaik, Sabita Prava (2009) found that government schools show highly satisfactory result in participative decision making than that of private and all the schools. Government, private and all the schools show the same status i.e. satisfactory in case of two dimensions, i.e. professional growth and supportive leadership.

Sharma, K.L. (1978) found that students having high intelligence had high self concept and high achievement. Self concept showed high positive and significant relationship with achievement and intelligence.

Sridhar, Y.N. and Hamid, Reza Badiei (2007) found that a high level of both emotional quotient and teacher efficacy would be correlated with student achievement, job satisfaction, teachers willingness to implement innovations, effective teaching. Emotional Quotient could be developed and increased through learning and experience in life span.

Suneetha, Sannidhi (2007) found that problem solving ability in physical science was at a low level in 10th class students. Telugu medium students had fewer problems solving ability when compared to English medium students who had more problem solving ability.

Tripathy, A.N. (1986) found that home and personality scores together predicted intelligence and achievement both in tribal and non-tribal groups.

Usha, P. and Sasi, Kumar (2007) reported that the correlation coefficient obtained for government and aided school teachers revealed that there is substantial correlation between teacher commitment and job satisfaction for government teachers but low and slight correlation for aided school teachers.

Vasanthi, A. (2008) found significant difference between the mean scores of group spirit of the teachers with respect to the type of the school and community involvement of the teachers with respect to the type of school.

Venkata, Ramana (2007) found no significant difference in professional competence between B.Ed. and TTC qualified secondary school teachers, B.Ed. and M.Ed. qualified secondary school teachers.

## Intelligence-Personality and Adjustment

Chamundeswari, S. and Vasanthi, S. (2009) reported that the central board school teachers are significantly better in their occupational commitment when compared to state board teachers and the matriculation teachers. Job satisfaction and occupational commitment are positively correlated with each other and significant at 0.01 level.

Dubey (1980) reported that intelligent frustrated subjects showed a high degree of conflict more displacement and a low degree of motivation as compared to normal frustrated group.

Dubey, R. (1984) reported that psychotics were hostile, day-dreaming, doubtful, mistrusting, interested in internal neutral life, low in intelligence, pessimistic, shy and withdrawing. Neurotics were simple enquiring regarding ideas, slow to learn and grasp, anxious, socially group dependent and uncontrolled. Normals are good natured, easy going, emotionally matured, cheerful, relaxed, satisfied and intelligent.

Nabi, Ahmed and Abdul, Rahman (2003) reported that there would be a significant relationship between criterion variable academic achievement and the predictive variable adjustment.

Rai, N.K. (1988) reported that blind subjects were less adjustable on the dimensions of family relationship, emotional stability, and adjustment to reality, mood and conformity.

Singh, Y. (1978) reported that average group showed a significant better adjustment on characteristic trait of personality than the superior group.

Sr. Eve, Justina Remould (2006) found difference in the impact of intervention programme to the experimental group and no such improvement was seen in the control group. Intervention programme was effective in terms of ability to build a healthy relationship with others.

## Intelligence-Personality and Age

Asthana, Anju (1989) found that social maturity increased with increase in grade level, the growth rate being highest in the first school year. Intelligence, academic achievement and adult-dependence were significantly associated with social maturity of child, although adult dependence had a negative association.

Bansibihari, Pandit (2004) found the level of emotional intelligence to be low and emotional quotient to be independent of age in secondary teachers.

Bharathi, K. (1988) found a developmental trend in casual thinking with increase in age. 5 year old children were not found to be at the comprehension stage. 8 year old children were found to be at the transactional stage, whereas 11 year old children were found to be at the logical thinking stage.

Kauser (1982) found no significant relationship between curiosity and intelligence on an overall basis except for girls of 10 years of age. The multiple correlation between curiosity and intelligence; creativity, extraversion and neuroticism for different age groups indicated overall significant relationship.

Swami, Priyankant M. (1989) found that the intelligence of orphan and normal students of ages 16, 17 and 18 was similar.

Vidhu, M. (1968) found that intelligence and extraversion were not related significantly, but introverts in the age group of 20 to 25 years were better on the Raven's Progressive Matrices. The neurotic students took much time on the Raven's Progressive Matrices than the extroverts.

## Intelligence-Personality and Attitude

Anantha, Lakshmi (2005) showed low negative thinking among students at intermediate level. There was no significant difference in negative thinking of day scholars and hostelers, English and Telugu medium students.

Arockiadoss, S. and Karumathur (2006) showed factors like attitude, attention and discipline to improve learning effectiveness among the college students.

Bhushan, L.I. (1968) showed that personality factors were substantially related to the leadership preference. Preference for a democratic type of leadership was positively related to extraversion and negatively to neuroticism, authoritarian type were submissive, intolerant of ambiguity, introvert and neurotic.

Kohli, Om Prakash (1989) showed that students belonging to high intelligence group and high SES were more religious in attitude than the students of the low intelligence group and low SES group. There was significant correlation between personality traits like intelligence, sober or enthusiastic, super-ego-strength, timid or venturesome, tough or tender minded, group dependent or self sufficient, self concept, self control and attitude scores of boys and girls in respect of religion.

Mishra, G. Santwana (2007) showed a strong positive correlation between attitudes of trainee teachers towards teaching profession.

## Intelligence-Personality and Creativity

Anderson and Cropley (1966) found that high creative thinkers were significantly more willing to take intellectual risk.

Iwata (1968) studied relationship of creativity with intelligence and personality variables and found that in the upper half of an intelligence test but in the lower half on the creativity test, the subjects were more independent, introverted and dominant but less sociable than those in the lower half in intelligence but in the upper half in the creativity. Those high on creativity test were relatively more extroverted and less neurotic.

Muddu, V. (1980) reported that high creative boys were emotionally controlled and self-assured.

Rani, R. (1986) reported that relationship between creativity and emotional stability as well as curiosity was dependent on intelligence.

Sen Gupta, M. (1979) reported that high creatives were more tolerant of ambiguity than low creatives. Intelligence was significantly correlated with total creativity.

Sunil, Dutt (2001) reported a significant correlation between creativity and problem solving ability, field dependent cognitive style and field independent cognitive style and creativity; field dependent, field independent and creativity.

## Intelligence-Personality and Gender

Anantha, Lakshmi (2005) reported a significant difference in negative thinking of boys and girls at intermediate level. Boys had more negative thinking than girls.

Arockiadoss, S. and Karumathur (2006) reported no difference in learning effectiveness among men and women students and day scholars and hostel students.

Asthana, Anju (1989) reported that sex did not present a consistent picture of its association with social maturity at different grade levels. Sex was not found to be related to social maturity except in Grades II and III where as girls were found to be more mature socially than boys.

Bansibihari, Pandit and Lata, Surwade (2006) reported no sex difference in emotionally mature group with respect to teacher effectiveness. Female teachers are emotionally more mature/stable than male teachers.

Bansibihari, Pandit (2004) found no significant difference in the level of emotional intelligence of male and female secondary teachers. The level of emotional intelligence is low and emotional quotient is independent of gender in secondary teachers.

Behera, Laxidhar (2004) found that women student teachers excelled their males in theory and practical performance.

Bhasin, Rajendra (1968) found disparity between the self-concept of male and female students while the boys showed a higher mean positive score in the area dealing with intelligence and emotional maturity, the girls showed higher mean positive score in the area of social achievement, aptitude and talent.

Bhatt, D.B. (1990) found that non-problematic male group were more intelligent and ego-strength than the problematic group. Female non-problematic group was found more intelligent and had higher ego-strength than female problematic group.

Chopra, Reeta and Gartia, Radhakanta (2009) found that there exists a significant difference in accountability of male and female secondary school teachers. Female teachers are more accountable towards their job as compared to male teachers.

Darsana, M. (2007) reported a significant difference between boys and girls in emotional understanding and emotional intelligence. There was no significant difference between boys and girls in emotional perception, emotional facilitation of thought and emotional management. Boys had higher means of emotional facilitation and emotional intelligence.

Fatima, Shaik (2005) reported a significant difference in the reasoning ability of boys and girls. Secondary school boys had high reasoning ability than secondary school girls.

George, M. (1969) reported that among student teachers men were more active and emotionally stable.

Gnanaguru, Selvaraj A. and Kumar, Suresh M. (2008) reported that the male and female students differ significantly in their home environment and attitude towards teaching and not in their achievement score and intelligence score.

John, Louis Manoharan and Christie, Doss (2007) reported that the emotional maturity of female P.G. students was higher than the male P.G. students.

Joshi, Renuka (1989) reported that females were higher on fluency, originality, extraversion and neuroticism than males.

Jyothi, Prathibha A. (2003) reported a significant difference in the independent problem solving ability of boys and girls in mathematics. Boys were significantly superior to that of girls in independent problem solving ability.

Konwar, L.N. (1989) reported that there was no significant difference in the levels of personal achievement motivation of boys and girls.

Kumari, Darshana (1986) found that intelligence and introversion were major contributors towards academic achievement of boys and intelligence and intellectual commitment were major contributors towards academic achievement of girls. No sex differences in intellectual commitment.

Laxmidhar, Behera and Sushant, Kumar (2004) found a significant difference in the performance of men and women student teachers in theory and practical subjects, women excelled more than women.

Madhavi, Yadla (2007) reported a significant difference between boys and girls in committing errors while attaining algebraic ability of class VIII, girls committed more errors than boys.

Magotra, H.P. (1982) reported that the mental health of boys and girls was influenced by intelligence and physical health.

Manoj, Kumar Dash (2005) reported that the predominant decision making style of men and women was found to be vigilance.

Mian, Shamshada (1988) reported that girls were superior to boys in intelligence and had higher score in achievement motivation. With intelligence as a constant variable, it was found that there were significant differences between boys with high intelligence and boys with low intelligence. High intelligent boys as compared to high intelligent girls were less neurotic, possessed realistic attitude and had hope of success. Low intelligent boys seemed to score higher in n-achievement, hope of success, perseverance and realistic attitude as compared to low intelligence girls.

Pal, Anitha (1988) reported that girls were more competitive than boys and no sex differences observed in cooperation.

Patel, S.S. (1982) reported no interaction effect between I.Q. and sex.

Patil, Ajaykimar Bhimrao (2006) reported no significant difference between emotional intelligence of male and female student teachers.

Ramesh, Mandalapu (2005) reported that there was no significant difference in the level of mathematical problem solving ability possessed by 9th class boys and girls of Telugu and English medium.

Ramesh, R. and Ponnambala, Thiagarajan A. (2005) reported no significant difference in self concept of the respondents in terms of their sex.

Ramganesh, E. (2006) reported no gender differences in emotional maturity.

Ramganesh, E. and Johnson, N. (2008) reported no significant mean difference in the gender of teacher educators' emotional quotient working in training colleges.

Selwyn, S. and Ben, Sam W. (2004) reported no significant difference between male and female D.T.Ed. students in self concept, vocabulary test, classification ability, spatial ability and attitude towards teaching profession.

Singh, K.K. (1985) reported that high intelligent girls were scholastic, controlled and shrewd. Low intelligent girls were outgoing, less scholastic and apprehensive. High intelligent males were scholastic, emotionally mature, conscientious, venturesome, tender minded, suspicious and controlled. Low intelligent males were outgoing, emotionally immature, assertive, happy-go-lucky, shrewd, imaginative, apprehensive, experimenting, self sufficient and tense.

Singh, Tirath and Kaur, Parminder (2008) found no significant effect of interaction between meditation and gender on self confidence when pre self confidence and pre general intelligence were taken as covariates.

Sinha, J.K.P. (1986) reported that high prejudiced males were tough-minded, outgoing, more intelligent, assertive, happy-go-lucky, controlled, tensed, and suspicious and had higher achievement motivation. High prejudiced females were slightly but significantly outgoing, more intelligent, assertive, tender minded, imaginative, experimenting, self sufficient, controlled, tensed and had higher achievement motivation.

Srivastava, P. (1981) reported that radical boys were more warm-hearted, more intelligent and more self-sufficient than conservative boys who were restless and excited, more reserved, less intelligent and less sufficient. Radical girls were more intelligent and had greater ego-strength, abundance surgency and frustration.

Subhashini, Y. (2005) reported no significant difference between the impact of peace education on emotional balance of boys and girls of secondary school.

Suneetha, Sannidhi (2007) reported no significant difference in problem solving ability in physical science between boys and girls of 10th class.

Suresh, K.J. and Joshith, V.P. (2008) reported that gender differences do not much matter in determining the level of emotional intelligence.

Swami, Priyankant M. (1989) reported that sex and grade had no effect on the differences in intelligence of orphan and normal students.

Usha, P. and Sasi, Kumar (2007) reported low and slight correlation between teacher's commitment and job satisfaction in case of male and female teachers.

Venkata, Ramana (2007) reported that there is no significant difference between male and female secondary school teachers in their professional competence.

### Intelligence-Personality and Home Background

Anantha, Lakshmi (2005) observed that pressure of parents is a cause for negative thinking.

Barlinge (1977) observed that children of emotionally balanced mothers tended to be less hostile than those of mothers making emotional balance. Children of prudent mothers were less negativistic and less hostile to parents than those of least prudent mothers. Children of sanguine mothers appeared to be relaxed whereas to those of less sanguine mothers tended to be tensed.

Jyothi, Prathibha A. (2003) observed a significant difference in the independent problem solving ability of residential and non-residential students. Residential school students have high independent problem solving ability than non-residential school students.

Pal, Anitha (1988) observed that the orientation of the father did not affect the cooperative or competitive disposition of their children.

### Intelligence-Personality and Locality

Arockiadoss, S. and Karumathur (2006) found that students of private, autonomous and urban colleges are more effective in learning and students of autonomous colleges and colleges offering above PG courses are more disciplined and attentive in learning.

Bansihihari, Pandit and Lata, Surwade (2006) found that urban teachers are found to be emotionally immature and unstable.

Bhatt, D.B. (1990) found that male rural non-problematic group had more general capacity and insight than male rural problematic group. Male rural non problematic group were more intelligent than male urban problematic group. Female urban non-problematic group was found socially precise, possessed more with power than female urban problematic group.

Bhatttacaryya, Anjana (1989) found that rural girls were the poorest group in aptitudes and scholastic achievement.

Darsana, M. (2007) found that emotional intelligence was high for rural students than urban students. Emotional intelligence was high for private than government school students.

Fatima, Shaik (2005) found a significant difference in the reasoning ability of rural and urban areas. Urbans had high reasoning ability than rurals.

Jhag (1979) found no significant difference in the pattern of personality correlates of creative children from urban and semi urban areas.

Jyothi, Prathibha A. (2003) found no significant difference in the independent problem solving ability of rural and urban students at secondary school level. Government school students had high independent problem solving ability than private school students but both were with average problem solving ability.

Khiangte, Varparhi (1988) found that rural high creative students when compared to urban high creative girls showed that high creative girls from urban areas were found to be more intelligent, emotionally stable, tender minded and self sufficient against their reserved group dependent and expedient rural counter parts.

Konwar, L.N. (1989) found no significant difference in the mean n-personal achievement scores of urban and rural residents.

Madhavi, Yadla (2007) found no significant difference between pupils of different localities in committing errors while attaining algebraic ability of class VIII.

Madhosh, A.G. (1989) found that the Kashmiri populars personality appeared to possess strong emotional stability, spontaneous and high mental ability, relaxed and they were not frustrated. The neglectees tended to be hard obstructives, dull and timid. The isolates were cool, generally tensed and restless. In Jammu sample affectionate, intelligent, self sufficient, aggressive and happy go-lucky. Neglectees were hard, obstructive, dull, timid, maladjusted but not submissive. The isolates were cool, dull, worldly wise, emotionally less stable but pessimistic. In Ladakh sample distinctly cool, wise, strictly conventional, conservative, slaves of their own urges, rule bounded and were not socially bold. The neglectees were the free thinking type, not conventional, participating, easy going, socially bold but guilt prove and emotionally stable but dull.

Patel, S.S. (1982) found no interaction effect between I.Q. and area variables.

Ramesh Mandalapu (2005) found that there was a significant difference in the level of mathematical problem solving ability possessed by rural and urban, urbans high than rurals and government low than private students of 9th class.

Ramesh, R. and Ponnambala, Thiagarajan A. (2005) reported no significant difference in self concept of the respondents in terms of their locality.

Ramganesh, E. (2006) found significant difference in emotional maturity of teacher trainee students belonging to urban and rural areas, rural area students had greater emotional maturity.

Singh, B.K. (1984) found high significant difference in the adjustment levels of rural and urban students. Rural students significantly more adjusted than urban students in home adjustment, social, school/college, health and emotional adjustment. In the area of social work and activities, no significant differences were discovered.

Subhashini, Y. (2005) reported no significant difference between the impact of peace education on emotional balance of rural and urban, English medium and Telugu medium secondary students.

Suneetha, Sannidhi (2007) reported no significant difference in problem solving ability in physical science between rural and urban and government and private students of 10th class.

Suri, Ishwar Saran (1989) reported that for the rural group, cognition of semantic classes, cognition of semantic relation and convergent production of semantic implications emerged as factors accounting for reasoning ability. For the urban group, convergent production of semantic classes emerged as the only factor to account for reasoning ability.

Tripathi, R.C. (1986) reported that urban science boys were generally better adjusted.

Usha, P. and Sasi, Kumar (2007) reported that teachers commitment and job satisfaction are substantially related in the case of rural school teachers but there exists no significant relation between teachers commitment and job satisfaction for urban teachers.

Venkata, Ramana (2007) found no significant difference between rural and urban school teachers in professional competence. Mean of rural teachers was higher than urban teachers.

## Intelligence-Personality and Religion

Ramesh, R. and Ponnambala, Thiagarajan A. (2005) reported no significant difference in self concept of the respondents in terms of their community.

Ramganesh, E. (2006) reported no significant difference in emotional maturity of students belonging to minority and non-minority levels.

Singh, Tirath and Kaur, Parminder (2008) reported no significant effect of interaction between meditation and religion on self confidence when pre general intelligence and pre general self confidence were taken as covariates.

Swami, Priyankant M. (1989) reported that the intelligence of normal Muslim students and orphan Muslim students was similar.

## Intelligence-Personality and Socio-economic Status (SES)

Asthana, Anju (1989) found no significant association between social maturity and SES of the child.

Darsana, M. (2007) found that emotional intelligence was high for high socio-economic status. There was no relation between emotional intelligence and socio-economic status for girls and private institutions.

Nabi, Ahmed and Abdul, Rahman (2003) found that there would be a significant relationship between criterion variable academic achievement and the predictive variable socio-economic status.

Pal, Anitha (1988) found that lower class subjects were more cooperative as well as competitive, followed by the middle and the upper classes.

Santosh and Kaur, Ravdeep (2009) reported that there is no significant difference between high and average SES students on scientific, executive, commercial, constructive, artistic, agricultural, persuasive, social and household areas.

On the other hand, there is significant difference between them in the area of literary interests. There is no significant difference between average and low SES students on literary, executive, commercial, constructive, artistic, agricultural, persuasive, social and household areas. On the other hand, there is significant difference between them in the area of scientific interests.

Sharma, K.L. (1978) found that students having high intelligence had high self concept and high socio-economic status.

Tripathy, A.N. (1986) reported that canonical correlation revealed the high SES with parental support, promotion of social personal maturity, educational stimulation and rejective control on children were associated with high intelligence, reflectiveness and a lesser degree of enthusiasm.

## Intelligence-Personality and Values

Agarwal, R. (1985) observed that personality was not related with moral development.

Chinara, B.D. (1992) observed that the self-confrontation strategy was found to be more effective than the clarifying-response strategy for inculcating the values of .equality, openness to reason, responsibility and co-operation.

Vasanthi, A. (2008) observed significant relationship between the decision making style of headmistresses and teacher morale.

So, to fill up the research gap existing in the field of intelligence and personality related to prospective teachers, this study was undertaken to identify the levels of intelligence and personality in prospective teachers and find out the correlation between intelligence and personality of prospective teachers.

Chapter

# 3

# Research Methodology

"Whatever you think, that you will be. If you think yourselves weak, weak you will be; if you think yourselves strong, strong you will be."

***— Swami Vivekananda***

## Method of Research

Research is a systematic enquiry seeking facts through objective verifiable methods in order to discover the relationship among them and to deduce from them the broad principles or laws. Therefore, the very success of a research work depends upon collecting the necessary information. Several methods of collecting information are developed to assist the research. Every survey expert has his own ideas of selecting the best method of collecting information. But, it cannot be uniform to all. Selection of the method depends on the type of information to be gathered and the sources of information to be consulted. For the present study, normative survey method is chosen.

Survey means viewing and interpreting things rigorously and comprehensively. Now-a-days, survey method is a popular way of collecting data and analyzing the results statistically and systematically. This method is suitable to this study as this one is a status study.

## OPERATIONAL DEFINITIONS OF KEY TERMS

The operational definitions of the important key terms used in the present study on "A Study of Anxiety of Prospective Teachers" are discussed and defined herewith:

- **Study:** Study refers to a systematic investigation which is objective and research oriented.
- **Prospective Teachers:** Student teacher's studying in Colleges of Education.
- **Intelligence:** Intelligence is the aggregate or global capacity of an individual to act purposefully, to think rationally and to deal effectively with his environment.
- **Personality:** Personality is the dynamic organization within the individual of those psycho-physical systems that determines his unique adjustment to the environment.
- **Gender:** Gender refers to male and female prospective teachers.
- **Locality:** Locality refers to rural and urban areas.
- **Methodology:** Methodology refers to the method of study under which the student has been admitted into the course. For the present study, arts and science teaching methodologies were considered.
    - Arts methodology, where in the student studies Social Studies as the elective subject.
    - Science methodology, where in the student studies Biological Science or Mathematics or Physical Science as the elective subject.
- **Educational Qualification:** Educational qualification refers to whether the student is a graduate or a post-graduate. For the present study, arts graduates and post-graduates and science graduates and post-graduates were considered.
    - *Graduates:* Those who have completed their three years course of study in arts or science or commerce as a specialized subject.

- *Post-Graduates:* Those who have completed their two years course of study in arts or science or commerce as a specialized subject.

## VARIABLES OF THE STUDY

Variables are the conditions or characteristics that the experimenter manipulates, controls or observes. There are mainly three types of variables, namely, independent, dependent and intervening. The independent variables are those variables which do not change on manipulation by the experimenter. The dependent variables are those variables which change on manipulation done by the experimenter. The intervening variables are those variables which are dependent both on dependent and independent variables.

For the present study, the following independent variables are chosen:

- *Gender:* Male and Female Prospective Teachers.
- *Locality:* Rural and Urban Prospective Teachers.
- *Methodology:* Arts and Science Prospective Teachers.
- *Educational Qualification:* Graduate and Post-Graduate Prospective Teachers.

It was found in the previous studies that there existed and as well as not existed significant difference in the intelligence and personality of males and females. So, to know if any difference exists in this study also, the variable 'gender' was considered.

It was found in the previous studies that there existed and as well as not existed significant difference in the intelligence and personality of rural and urban students. So, to know if any difterence exists in this study also, the variable 'locality' was considered.

It was found in the previous studies that there existed and not existed a significant difference in the intelligence and personality of arts and science students. So, to know if any difference exists in this study also, the variable 'methodology' was considered.

Since no previous studies were conducted on the variable namely educational qualification, to know if any difference exists, in this study the variable educational qualification was considered.

It was found in the previous studies that there existed and not existed an association between intelligence and personality of male and female, urban and rural, arts and science and graduate and post-graduate students. So, to know if any association/correlation exists in this study also, the variables 'gender', 'locality', 'methodology of study' and 'educational qualification' was considered.

## HYPOTHESES OF THE STUDY

Hypothesis is a tentative generalization which provides basis to the whole study to be tested by facts. It is a shrewd and intelligent guess, supposition, inference, hunch, provisional statement, a tentative generalization to the existence of some fact, condition or relationship relative to some phenomena which serves to explain already known facts in a given area of knowledge and which guides the search for new truth on the basis of empirical evidence.

In statistical hypothesis, the sample should be representative of the whole population. This can be ensured in random sampling where the units of population have got equal chances of being represented. The hypothesis to be tested in this study is 'null hypothesis.' Ordinarily, a null hypothesis is a statement to believe that there is no relation to the independent and dependent variable. Once it is formulated, depending on the outcome, it will be either accepted or rejected. For the present study the following hypotheses were framed.

*Hypothesis 1.* There is no very superior intelligence in prospective teachers.

*Hypothesis 1A*. There is no significant difference in the intelligence of male and female prospective teachers.

*Hypothesis 1B*. There is no significant difference in the intelligence of rural and urban prospective teachers.

*Hypothesis 1C*. There is no significant difference in the intelligence of arts and science prospective teachers.

*Hypothesis 1D*. There is no significant difference in the intelligence of graduate and post-graduate prospective teachers.

*Hypothesis 2*. There is no emotionally well balanced personality in prospective teachers.

*Hypothesis 2A*. There is no significant difference in the personality of male and female prospective teachers.

*Hypothesis 2B*. There is no significant difference in the personality of rural and urban prospective teachers.

*Hypothesis 2C*. There is no significant difference in the personality of arts and science prospective teachers.

*Hypothesis 2D*. There is no significant difference in the personality of graduate and post-graduate prospective teachers.

*Hypothesis 3*. There is no correlation between intelligence and personality of prospective teachers.

*Hypothesis 3A*. There is no correlation between intelligence and personality of male and female prospective teachers.

*Hypothesis 3B*. There is no correlation between intelligence and personality of rural and urban prospective teachers.

*Hypothesis 3C*. There is no correlation between intelligence and personality of arts and science prospective teachers.

*Hypothesis 3D*. There is no correlation between intelligence and personality of graduate and post-graduate prospective teachers.

## SAMPLE OF THE STUDY

A sample is a smaller representation of the larger whole. A sample contains primarily sampling units and a slice of the population representing the universe. A sample must possess the following essential characteristics to provide accurate results. They are representativeness, adequacy, and homogeneity, lack of bias, smallness in size, accuracy and completeness.

As a sample is a slice of the population, the population for the study refers to all the prospective teachers who undergo one year study during their B.Ed. course in the Colleges of Education of Ranga Reddy district.

Sampling is the easiest method of social investigation. The purpose of sampling is to draw inferences concerning the universe. There are three elements in the process of sampling. They are selection of the sample, collection of information and drawing inferences. According to Cornell, "sampling is the process by which a relatively small number of individuals are selected or analyzed in order to find out something about the entire population or the universe from which it is selected". In any research, various methods are utilized for selection of samples. After a detailed study of all the methods, the stratified random sampling method was selected for the present study.

In the stratified sampling method, the entire population will be divided into smaller homogeneous groups or strata, and then a sample is selected within each group. Every sampling unit in the population is placed in one of the strata prior to the selection of the sample so that the sum of the strata is identical with the population.

Stratified sampling method has certain merits as a technique of sampling. Auckoff has rightly said that stratified sampling enables the researcher to make a composition of properties of the strata as well as to estimate population characteristics.

In this stratified sampling method, the investigator will have greater control over the selection of the sample when compared with random sampling. In random sampling, although every group has a chance of being selected and included in the sample, there is every possibility, and sometimes it does happen, that certain important groups are left unrepresented. But, in stratified sampling method, no important group is likely to be left out.

Stratified sampling method is the ideal one when comparison between different variables has to be made. For example, if comparison has to be made between men and women prospective teachers or rural and urban prospective teachers, it would be very difficult to select the required number of units through any other method of sampling. If any other method is used, the problem of bias and prejudice creeps in.

Replacement of units is also possible in the stratified sampling method. Normally, if a particular unit is not accessible for a study, it is difficult to replace it by another, but in this method it is possible. Stephen states that stratification automatically brings about a replacement of persons lost in the sample, by persons of the same stratum, thus partly correcting the bias that would result if there were no replacement of losses. As the entire population is divided into particular strata, it is easy and convenient to replace an inaccessible case by an accessible one.

In stratified sampling method, much depends on stratification process. The following precautions were taken while stratifying the population. The variables involved in the study were taken note of; care was taken to see that each stratum in the universe was large enough in size so that selection of items could be done on random basis; the strata formed were definite and clear cut; each stratum was free from influence of the other; and there was no overlapping.

Before actually selecting the sample, certain fundamental principles were considered to make the sample scientific and clear cut (Bhaskara Rao, 1989).

*Firstly,* the 'universe' was clearly defined. In the technical phraseology of research, the whole population out of which the samples are selected is known as the 'universe'. For the present research work, the universe includes all the secondary school science teachers working in secondary schools of Andhra Pradesh. The study was limited to a particular geographical area to facilitate appropriate sample selection and to avoid wastage of time and money.

*Secondly*, decision was made about the units of the sample. A unit of sample may he a house, a family, a group of individuals or a single individual. A good unit should possess the following characteristics: 1. *Clarity*: The unit should be clearly defined in unambiguous terms. This would make the study easy and efficient. For the present research work, a sampling unit is defined as a prospective teacher studying in any College of Education of Ranga Reddy district; 2. *Suitability*: A good unit should be well suited to the problem under study. Since the problem is the study of the intelligence and personality of the prospective teachers, the unit selected is well suited to the problem; 3. *Accessibility*: The unit selected should be easily accessible to the researcher. If the units selected are difficult to reach and if the researcher fails to make use of them, the study would be vitiated. The selected sampling units, i.e., prospective teachers, are easily accessible since they could be approached in any College of Education.

*Thirdly*, availability of sample and preparation of the source list are very much essential. This is an important factor that makes representative selection possible. A source list is the list which contains the names of the units of the universe from which the sample may be selected. It may exist even before the beginning of the project or it may be prepared afresh by the investigator himself. Without a source list, study through sampling method is not possible. For the present research work, a source list consisting of the names of Colleges of Education in the Ranga Reddy district is used. Care was taken to see that the source list was up-to-date and valid and that there was no repetition of names of the schools. This source list was found to be relevant and suitable because it included

College of Education as the study deals with the intelligence and personality of prospective teachers.

Besides considering these principles, it is extremely important to think about the size of the sample to be selected. If the sample is either too small or too large, it will make the study difficult and the results untenable. According to Parten, "An optimum sample in survey is one which fulfils the requirements of effective representatives, reliability and flexibility. The sample should be small enough to avoid intolerable sampling error." The size of sample (Bhaskara Rao, 1989) for the present research work was decided after considering the following factors:

- ➢ Since an intensive study was planned, a very large number of samples were not selected. In the case of an intensive study, employing a very large number of samples is not very useful as it involves huge consumption of resources. A smaller sample will be more convenient.
- ➢ The size and selection of the samples are also influenced by the nature of the universe. If the universe is homogeneous, even a small-sized sample may yield dependable and required results. If the universe is heterogeneous, small-sized samples may not be useful. In the case of the present study, the heterogeneous universe was split into smaller homogeneous strata and then the samples were selected from these strata. For example, the prospective teachers of Ranga Reddy district were broadly grouped under men and women, and rural and urban prospective teachers. A sample was selected from each of these groups.
- ➢ The researcher needs to determine the number of groups to be formed. In case the number of groups proposed is large, the size of the samples shall have to be large so that every group would be of proper size and suit the requirements of the study; in case the

number of groups proposed is small, even small-sized samples can fulfill the requirement. In the case of the present study, the universe was divided into male and female prospective teachers, rural and urban prospective teachers, graduate and post-graduate prospective teachers, arts and science prospective teachers, etc. Since the number of groups was moderate, a reasonable sample was selected from each of these groups.

➢ Practical considerations and accuracy will also play a vital role in determining the size of the sample. Every study is guided by certain practical considerations such as time, resources, accessibility of the data, etc. Generally, it is believed that a large-sized sample is more representative and usually produces accurate results. This, of course, mainly depends upon the technique of sampling used. If the sampling technique is scientific, even small-sized samples can produce dependable and accurate results. While selecting the size of the sample for the present study, practical considerations like the availability of resources and time were taken into consideration. Care was taken to make the sample selection technique as scientific as possible.

➢ The size of the sample is also governed by the size of the tools to be used. In case the tools are short and the questions asked pertain to certain limited factors, a large sample can be selected. In case the tools are large and the questions complicated, the sample should be small in size so that, from administrative point of view, the researcher may not be put to unnecessary troubles. In the present study, as the tools were quite elaborate and need careful attention of the sample, a very large sample was not selected.

➢ The sampling method also determines the size of the sample. When random sampling method is used, the samples have to be large. On the other hand, if samples are selected through stratified sampling method, the reliability can be achieved even with the help of small-sized samples.

Taking these factors that influence the size of the sample into consideration, it was decided that an ideal sample would consist of 600 prospective teachers. This sample is small enough to avoid unnecessary troubles and large enough to avoid intolerable sampling errors.

After deciding about the sampling method, the universe selected was divided into different strata. The variables chosen for the study were considered in dividing the universe. The sampling design employed here involved not only the stratification of the universe but also the random sampling technique to select the samples from within the stratum.

In order to reduce the sampling error the sample size of 600 was chosen. In this study, the strata divided are represented in the following table:

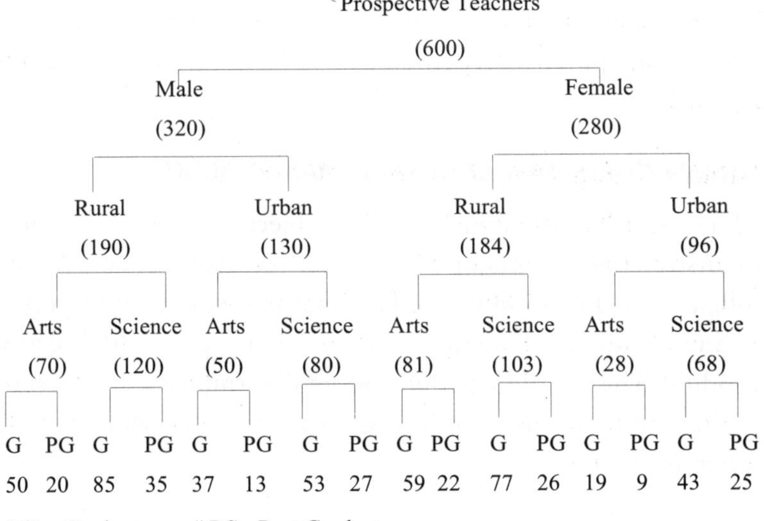


# G – Graduates # PG - Post Graduates

## TOOLS OF THE STUDY

A research tool is a tool which has reliability and validity. It is used for the purpose of data collection. Reliability is the degree of consistency that the instrument or procedure demonstrates. Validity is that quality of a data gathering instrument or procedure which enables it to measure what it is supposed to measure.

A research tool plays a major role in worthwhile research, as it is the sole factor in determining sound data and in arriving at perfect conclusions about the problem or study in hand, which ultimately helps in providing suitable remedial measures to the problem concerned. The selection and use of tool can be done in two ways. The first one is to construct a tool independently by the researcher and the second one is to select a standardized tool that is already available in the field of study.

The tools used in the present study are 'The Group Test of General Mental Ability (20-52)' standardized by S. Jalota and 'Personality Inventory Scale' standardized by Eysenck.

### Jalota's Group Test of General Mental Ability

Jalota's test has 100 items and the subject is given 25 minutes to answer these items or this test can be given in an average college period of 45 minutes. The total score can be interpreted as a grade on an 11-point C-scale or on a 7-point Intelligence Grading. The centile position can be determined by reference to the centile norms. A useful IQ Reckoner is provided for the range 60 to 140.

**Tables giving Norms**

| 1. C Scale | | 2. Centile norms | | 3. I.Q. Reckoner | |
|---|---|---|---|---|---|
| Grade | Range | Percentile | Score | I.Q. | Score |
| 10 | 88+ | 97 | 84+ | 140 | 85 |
| 9 | 80 – 87 | 95 | 77 – 83 | 130 | 80 |
| 8 | 71 – 79 | 90 | 72 – 76 | 125 | 76 |
| 7 | 63 – 70 | 80 | 67 – 71 | 120 | 72 |
| 6 | 55 – 62 | 75 | 64 – 66 | 115 | 68 |
| 5 | 47 – 54 | 70 | 62 – 63 | 110 | 64 |
| 4 | 39 – 46 | 60 | 57 – 61 | 105 | 58 |
| 3 | 31 – 38 | 50 | 53 – 56 | 100 | 51 |
| 2 | 23 – 30 | 40 | 48 – 52 | 95 | 46 |
| 1 | 15 – 22 | 30 | 43 – 47 | 90 | 40 |
| 0 | 0 – 14 | 25 | 40 – 42 | 85 | 34 |
| | | 20 | 36 – 39 | 80 | 28 |
| | | 16 | 27 – 35 | 75 | 24 |
| | | 5 | 22 – 26 | 70 | 19 |
| | | 2 | 16 – 21 | 65 | 15 |
| | | | | 60 | 10 |

**Table giving Intelligence Grades**

| P.E. | Score | Grade |
|---|---|---|
| +3+ | 85+ | Very Superior |
| +2 to +3 | 73 – 84 | Superior |
| +1 to +2 | 62 – 73 | Bright Average |
| -1 to +1 | 40 – 62 | Average |
| -1 to -2 | 29 – 40 | Dull Average |
| -2 to -3 | 18 – 29 | Borderline |
| -3 below | 0 – 17 | Mental Defect |

## *Scoring*

Scoring is an important process in the research, as the outcomes of the research are based on the scoring procedure. For the present study the scoring done is as follows :

**Jalota Test of Intelligence**

| Sl. No. | Score | Sl. No. | Score | Sl. No. | Score | Sl. No. | Score |
|---|---|---|---|---|---|---|---|
| 1 | 2 | 26 | 5 | 51 | 5 | 76 | 3 |
| 2 | 4 | 27 | 7 | 52 | 3 | 77 | 5 |
| 3 | 3 | 28 | 3 | 53 | 2 | 78 | 1 |
| 4 | 1 | 29 | 5 | 54 | 3 | 79 | 2 |
| 5 | 3 | 30 | 1 | 55 | 1 | 80 | 5 |
| 6 | 4 | 31 | 3 | 56 | 5 | 81 | 1 |
| 7 | 5 | 32 | 4 | 57 | 3 | 82 | 4 |
| 8 | 2 | 33 | 6 | 58 | 3 | 83 | 4 |
| 9 | 4 | 34 | 5 | 59 | 4 | 84 | 3 |
| 10 | 1 | 35 | 1 | 60 | 1 | 85 | 6 |
| 11 | 1 | 36 | 4 | 61 | 3 | 86 | 5 |
| 12 | 5 | 37 | 3 | 62 | 1 | 87 | 4 |
| 13 | 4 | 38 | 7 | 63 | 5 | 88 | 3 |
| 14 | 2 | 39 | 4 | 64 | 2 | 89 | 5 |
| 15 | 1 | 40 | 3 | 65 | 4 | 90 | 4 |
| 16 | 4 | 41 | 1 | 66 | 2 | 91 | 3 |
| 17 | 2 | 42 | 4 | 67 | 3 | 92 | 2 |
| 18 | 4 | 43 | 5 | 68 | 4 | 93 | 3 |
| 19 | 3 | 44 | 1 | 69 | 5 | 94 | 1 |
| 20 | 3 | 45 | 3 | 70 | 4 | 95 | 8 |
| 21 | 4 | 46 | 1 | 71 | 1 | 96 | 2 |
| 22 | 1 | 47 | 5 | 72 | 5 | 97 | 5 |
| 23 | 2 | 48 | 4 | 73 | 3 | 98 | 1 |
| 24 | 5 | 49 | 5 | 74 | 4 | 99 | 4 |
| 25 | 4 | 50 | 3 | 75 | 7 | 100 | 3 |

## EYSENCK'S PERSONALITY INVENTORY

Eysenck Personality Inventory is the briefest and the most popular Inventory among all the personality Inventories. It has 57 questions out of which 24 questions measure Introversion-Extroversion, 24 questions measure Stability-Instability and 9 questions measure the tendency to lie. An extroverted person is carefree, easy going and optimistic. An introverted person is a quiet, retiring sort of a person who keeps his feelings under control. A stable person is even tempered, calm and lively whereas an unstable person is anxious, moody, touchy and restless. An understanding of the personality helps in vocational and educational guidance.

### Interpretation of Values

- 17 and above Extrovert
- 7 and below Introvert
- 14 and above Neurotic
- 4 and below emotionally well balanced
- If the total Lie Score is 5 and above reject the data.

## ADMINISTRATION OF THE TOOLS

The tools were administered personally by one of the researches on the prospective teachers and the sample was asked to respond to the statements. Before giving the tools to the participants, the researcher explained the purpose of the present investigation. Directions given on the cover sheet were read out to the participants and specific instructions were given. Then the sample answered the scale.

## Chapter

# 4

# Analysis of the Data

"You are the creator of your own destiny."

*— Swami Vivekananda*

Analysis of the data is the most skilled task of all stages of research. It depends on the judgement and skill of the researcher. It should be done by the researcher and should not be entrusted to another person. Analysis of data means studying the tabulated material in order to determine inherent facts or meanings. It involves breaking down complex factors into simple ones and putting the parts in new arrangements for the purpose of interpretation.

The first step in the analysis of data is a critical examination of the assembled data. This includes the researcher to think and analyze the data in the next method of analysis, coding. Coding involves assigning symbols to each response, the purpose of which is to translate raw data into symbols. This depends on proper coding of responses. Coding can be done by the respondent or observer or the interviewer. There may be difficulties in coding due to inadequacy of data, inefficiency of the coder and lack of editing or scrutinizing of the available data. Editing can be helpful for coding and for improving the quality of data collection.

Tabulation is a means of recording classification in a compact form in such a way so as to facilitate comparisons. Data is arranged in rows and columns to facilitate mathematical and statistical operations. It is of great help in the analysis and interpretation of data. While tabulating the data, the purpose of the study has to be kept in mind.

The method of analysis chosen for a particular study depends upon the nature of objectives, hypotheses to be tested, the purpose and use of the study. Statistical methods are the mathematical techniques used to facilitate the interpretation of numerical data secured from groups of individuals or group of observations or a single individual. A basic knowledge about statistics becomes inevitable for research workers, for systematic analysis and accurate and precise interpretation of data.

For the present study titled, "A Study of Intelligence and Personality of Prospective Teachers", several statistical techniques were used to perform the analysis. After collecting the data from six hundred prospective teachers through standardized tools, the analysis was performed keeping in view objectives framed, hypotheses formulated, type of data collected, type of tools used, etc.

The highest intelligence score or the lowest intelligence score one can get is 100 or 0 respectively. The highest personality score or the lowest personality score one can get is 57 or 0 respectively. For this purpose, mean, standard deviation, critical ratio, etc., were employed.

### Hypothesis 1

*There is no very superior intelligence in prospective teachers.*

To test the validity of hypothesis 1, the mean of the intelligence scores was calculated.

**Table 4.1 : Intelligence of Prospective Teachers**

| Sample | Size | Mean | Standard Deviation |
|---|---|---|---|
| Whole | 600 | 66.96 | 9.28 |

From the mean value of table 4.1, it is evident that there was a bright average level of intelligence in prospective teachers.

The hypothesis that "there is no very superior intelligence in prospective teachers" can be rejected as the prospective teachers possess a bright average level of intelligence.

## Hypothesis 1A

*There is no significant difference in the intelligence of male and female prospective teachers.*

To test the validity of hypothesis 1A, the following calculations were carried out.

**Table 4.2 : Comparison of Intelligence Among Male and Female Prospective Teachers**

| Variable | Sample Size | Mean | S.D. | Mean Difference | Standard Error of Means | Critical Ratio |
|---|---|---|---|---|---|---|
| Male | 320 | 67.05 | 9.17 | 0.19 | 0.760 | 0.25* |
| Female | 280 | 66.86 | 9.42 | | | |

* Not Significant at 0.05 level

From the values of table 4.2, it is evident that the intelligence level in male and female prospective teachers was not significantly different, though both of them possess a bright average level of intelligence.

The hypothesis that "there is no significant difference in the intelligence of male and female prospective teachers" can be accepted as there is no significant difference in the level of intelligence of male and female prospective teachers.

### Hypothesis 1B

*There is no significant difference in the intelligence of rural and urban prospective teachers*

To test the validity of the hypothesis 1B, the following calculations were made.

**Table 4.3 : Comparison of Intelligence among Rural and Urban Prospective Teachers**

| Variable | Sample Size | Mean | S.D. | Mean Difference | Standard Error of Means | Critical Ratio |
|---|---|---|---|---|---|---|
| Rural | 374 | 65.46 | 9.79 | 3.98 | 0.723 | 5.50+ |
| Urban | 226 | 69.44 | 7.77 | | | |

+ Significant at 0.05 level

From the values of table 4.3, it is evident that the intelligence level in rural and urban prospective teachers was significantly different, though both of them possess a bright average level of intelligence.

The hypothesis that "there is no significant difference in the intelligence of rural and urban prospective teachers" can be rejected as there is a significant difference in the level of intelligence of rural and urban prospective teachers.

### Hypothesis 1C

*There is no significant difference in the intelligence of arts and science prospective teachers.*

To test the validity of hypothesis 4, the following calculations were carried out.

**Table 4.4 : Comparison of Intelligence among Arts and Science Prospective Teachers**

| Variable | Sample Size | Mean | S.D. | Mean Difference | Standard Error of Means | Critical Ratio |
|---|---|---|---|---|---|---|
| Arts teachers | 229 | 64.51 | 10.08 | 3.96 | 0.795 | 4.98+ |
| Science teachers | 371 | 68.47 | 8.41 | | | |

+ Significant at 0.05 level

From the values of table 4.4, it is evident that the intelligence level in arts and science prospective teachers was significantly different, though both of them possess a bright average level of intelligence.

The hypothesis that "there is no significant difference in the intelligence of arts and science prospective teachers" can be rejected as there is a significant difference in the level of intelligence of arts and science prospective teachers.

## Hypothesis 1D

*There is no significant difference in the intelligence of graduate and post-graduate prospective teachers.*

To test the validity of hypothesis 1D, the following calculations were calculated

**Table 4.5 : Comparison of Intelligence among Graduate and Post-graduate Prospective Teachers**

| Variable | Sample Size | Mean | S.D. | Mean Difference | Standard Error of Means | Critical Ratio |
|---|---|---|---|---|---|---|
| Graduates | 423 | 64.62 | 9.08 | 7.93 | 0.694 | 11.42+ |
| Post Graduates | 177 | 72.55 | 7.13 | | | |

+ Significant at 0.05 level

From the values of table 4.5, it is evident that the intelligence level in graduate and post-graduate prospective teachers was significantly different, though both of them possess a bright average level of intelligence.

The hypothesis that "there is no significant difference in the intelligence of graduate and post-graduate prospective teachers" can be rejected as there is a significant difference in the level of intelligence of graduate and post-graduate prospective teachers.

## Hypothesis 2

*There is no emotionally well balanced personality in prospective teachers.*

To test the validity of hypothesis 6, the mean of the personality scores was calculated.

**Table 4.6 : Personality of Prospective Teachers**

| Sample | Size | Mean | Standard Deviation |
|---|---|---|---|
| Whole | 600 | 42.73 | 4.97 |

From the mean value of table 4.6, it is evident that there was a highly extrovert personality in prospective teachers.

The hypothesis that "there is no emotionally well balanced personality in prospective teachers" can be rejected as the prospective teachers possess a highly extrovert personality.

## Hypothesis 2A

*There is no significant difference in the personality of male and female prospective teachers.*

To test the validity of hypothesis 2A, the following calculations were carried out.

**Table 4.7: Comparison of Personality among Male and Female Prospective Teachers**

| Variable | Sample Size | Mean | S.D. | Mean Difference | Standard Error of Means | Critical Ratio |
|---|---|---|---|---|---|---|
| Male | 320 | 42.72 | 4.91 | 0.03 | 0.407 | 0.073* |
| Female | 280 | 42.75 | 5.05 | | | |

*Not Significant at 0.05 level

From the values of table 4.7, it is evident that the personality level in male and female prospective teachers was not significantly different, though both of them possess a highly extrovert personality.

The hypothesis that "there is no significant difference in the personality of male and female prospective teachers" can be accepted as there is no significant difference in the level of personality of male and female prospective teachers.

## Hypothesis 2B

*There is no significant difference in the personality of rural and urban prospective teachers.*

To test the validity of the hypothesis 2B, the following calculations were made.

**Table 4.8 : Comparison of Personality among Rural and Urban Prospective Teachers**

| Variable | Sample Size | Mean | S.D. | Mean Difference | Standard Error of Means | Critical Ratio |
|---|---|---|---|---|---|---|
| Rural | 374 | 42.14 | 5.27 | 1.58 | 0.392 | 4.03+ |
| Urban | 226 | 43.72 | 4.26 | | | |

+ Significant at 0.05 level

From the values of table 4.8, it is evident that the personality level in rural and urban prospective teachers was significantly different, though both of them possess a highly extrovert personality.

The hypothesis that "there is no significant difference in the personality of rural and urban prospective teachers" can be rejected as there is a significant difference in the level of personality of rural and urban prospective teachers.

## Hypothesis 2C

*There is no significant difference in the personality of arts and science prospective teachers.*

To test the validity of hypothesis 2C, the following calculations were carried out.

**Table 4.9 : Comparison of Personality among Arts and Science Prospective Teachers**

| Variable | Sample Size | Mean | S.D. | Mean Difference | Standard Error of Means | Critical Ratio |
|---|---|---|---|---|---|---|
| Arts teachers | 229 | 41.90 | 5.21 | 1.35 | 0.423 | 3.191+ |
| Science teachers | 371 | 43.25 | 4.76 | | | |

+ Significant at 0.05 level

From the values of table 4.9, it is evident that the personality level in arts and science prospective teachers was significantly different, though both of them possess a highly extrovert personality.

The hypothesis that "there is no significant difference in the personality of arts and science prospective teachers" can be rejected as there is a significant difference in the level of personality of arts and science prospective teachers.

## Hypothesis 2D

*There is no significant difference in the personality of graduate and post-graduate prospective teachers.*

To test the validity of hypothesis 2D, the following calculations were calculated.

**Table 4.10 : Comparison of Personality among Graduate and Post-graduate Prospective Teachers**

| Variable | Sample Size | Mean | S.D. | Mean Difference | Standard Error of Means | Critical Ratio |
|---|---|---|---|---|---|---|
| Graduates | 423 | 41.82 | 4.97 | 3.1 | 0.399 | 7.769+ |
| Post Graduates | 177 | 44.92 | 4.24 | | | |

+ Significant at 0.05 level

From the values of table 4.10, it is evident that the personality level in graduate and post-graduate prospective teachers was significantly different, though both of them possess a highly extrovert personality.

The hypothesis that "there is no significant difference in the personality of graduate and post-graduate prospective teachers" can be rejected as there is a significant difference in the level of personality of graduate and post-graduate prospective teachers.

## Hypothesis 3

*There is no correlation between intelligence and personality of prospective teachers.*

To test the validity of hypothesis 3, the mean of the intelligence scores was calculated.

**Table 4.11 : Correlation between Intelligence and Personality of Prospective Teachers**

| Variable | Sample Size | Mean | S.D. | Correlation |
|---|---|---|---|---|
| Intelligence | 600 | 66.96 | 9.28 | 0.876 |
| Personality | 600 | 42.73 | 4.97 | |

From the correlation value of table 4.11, it is evident that there exists a high positive correlation between intelligence and personality of prospective teachers.

The hypothesis that "there is no correlation between intelligence and personality of prospective teachers" can be rejected as there is a high positive correlation between intelligence and personality of prospective teachers.

## Hypothesis 3A

*There is no correlation between intelligence and personality of male and female prospective teachers.*

To test the validity of hypothesis 3A, the following calculations were carried out.

**Table 4.12 : Correlation between Intelligence and Personality of Male and Female Prospective Teachers**

| Variable | | Sample Size | Mean | S.D. | Correlation |
|---|---|---|---|---|---|
| Male | Intelligence | 320 | 67.05 | 9.17 | 0.877 |
| | Personality | 320 | 42.72 | 4.91 | |
| Female | Intelligence | 280 | 66.86 | 9.42 | 0.876 |
| | Personality | 280 | 42.75 | 5.05 | |

From the correlation values of table 4.12, it is evident that there exists a high positive correlation between intelligence and personality of male and female prospective teachers.

The hypothesis that "there is no correlation between intelligence and personality of male and female prospective teachers" can be rejected as there is a high positive correlation between intelligence and personality of male and female prospective teachers.

## Hypothesis 3B

*There is no correlation between intelligence and personality of rural and urban prospective teachers.*

To test the validity of the hypothesis 3B, the following calculations were made.

**Table 4.13 : Correlation between Intelligence and Personality of Rural and Urban Prospective Teachers**

| Variable | | Sample Size | Mean | S.D. | Correlation |
|---|---|---|---|---|---|
| Rural | Intelligence | 374 | 65.46 | 9.79 | 0.851 |
| | Personality | 374 | 42.14 | 5.27 | |
| Urban | Intelligence | 226 | 69.44 | 7.77 | 0.932 |
| | Personality | 226 | 43.72 | 4.26 | |

From the correlation values of table 4.13, it is evident that there exists a high positive correlation between intelligence and personality of rural and urban prospective teachers.

The hypothesis that "there is no correlation between intelligence and personality of rural and urban prospective teachers" can be rejected as there is a high positive correlation between intelligence and personality of rural and urban prospective teachers.

## Hypothesis 3C

*There is no correlation between intelligence and personality of arts and science prospective teachers.*

To test the validity of hypothesis 3C, the following calculations were carried out.

**Table 4.14 : Correlation between Intelligence and Personality of Arts and Science Prospective Teachers**

| Variable | | Sample Size | Mean | S.D. | Correlation |
|---|---|---|---|---|---|
| Arts methodology | Intelligence | 229 | 64.51 | 10.08 | 0.520 |
| | Personality | 229 | 41.9 | 5.21 | |
| Science methodology | Intelligence | 371 | 68.47 | 8.41 | 0.883 |
| | Personality | 371 | 43.25 | 4.76 | |

From the correlation values of table 4.14, it is evident that there exists a moderate positive correlation between intelligence and personality of arts prospective teachers and a high positive correlation between intelligence and personality of science prospective teachers.

The hypothesis that "there is no correlation between intelligence and personality of arts methodology and science methodology prospective teachers" can be rejected as there is a moderate positive and high positive correlation respectively between intelligence and personality of arts and science prospective teachers.

## Hypothesis 3D

*There is no correlation between intelligence and personality of graduate and post-graduate prospective teachers.*

To test the validity of hypothesis 3D, the following calculations were calculated.

**Table 4.15 : Correlation of Intelligence and Personality of Graduate and Post-graduate Prospective Teachers**

| Variable | | Sample Size | Mean | S.D. | Correla-tion |
|---|---|---|---|---|---|
| Graduates | Intelligence | 423 | 64.62 | 9.08 | 0.866 |
| | Personality | 423 | 41.82 | 4.97 | |
| Post-graduates | Intelligence | 177 | 72.55 | 7.13 | 0.871 |
| | Personality | 177 | 44.92 | 4.24 | |

From the correlation values of table 4.15, it is evident that there exists a high positive correlation between intelligence and personality of graduate and post-graduate prospective teachers.

The hypothesis that "there is no correlation between intelligence and personality of graduate and post-graduate prospective teachers" can be rejected as there is a high positive correlation between intelligence and personality of graduate and post-graduate prospective teachers.

Chapter

# 5

# Summary, Conclusion and Discussion

"People are like stained-glass windows. They sparkle and shine when the sun is out, but when the darkness sets in their true beauty is revealed only if there is a light from within."

***— Elisabeth Kubler-Ross***

## SUMMARY

The prospective teachers are the teachers in making. They need good personality and high intelligence to meet the cognitive and affective need of students after becoming the teachers in secondary schools.

*Intelligence* is the ability of adjusting in a new situation. According to Wells, "Intelligence is the property of recombining our behaviour pattern so as to act better in a novel situation." In William Stern's opinion, "Intelligence is the ability to adjust oneself to a new situation." Intelligence is a general ability to adjust to new situations. Testing of intelligence started with Alfred Binet. A variety of intelligence tests have been designed by psychologists. They can be classified as: (*a*) Verbal Tests; (*b*) Non-verbal tests; and (*c*) Performance tests. Intelligence tests have also been grouped as individual tests and group tests. They can also be classified as power tests and speed tests.

The unique features of a person comprise his *personality.* No two individuals have the same personality. Fredenburgh in his book, the psychology of personality and adjustment, tried to synthesize all definitions and observed, "Personality is a stable system of complex characteristics by which the life pattern of the individual may be identified". An individual is characterized and distinguished from others by his personality. Personal appearance, Intelligence, Temperament, Character, Stability and Persistence are some of the essential traits of personality. Assessment of personality is one of the important contributions of psychology to human society.

The present study is confined to Ranga Reddy district. The sample was drawn from the prospective teachers studying in Colleges of Education. The sample size chosen for the present study was 600 prospective teachers.

The *objectives* of the study were: (1) To find out the intelligence of prospective teachers; (2) To find out the intelligence of male and female prospective teachers; (3) To find out the intelligence of rural and urban prospective teachers; (4) To find out the intelligence of arts and science prospective teachers; (5) To find out the intelligence of graduate and post-graduate prospective teachers; (6) To find out the personality of prospective teachers; (7) To find out the personality of male and female prospective teachers; (8) To find out the personality of rural and urban prospective teachers; (9) To find out the personality of arts and science prospective teachers; (10) To find out the personality of graduate and post-graduate prospective teachers; (11) To find out the correlation between intelligence and personality of prospective teachers; (12) To find out the correlation between intelligence and personality of male and female prospective teachers; (13) To find out the correlation between intelligence and personality of rural and urban prospective teachers; (14) To find out the correlation between intelligence and personality of arts and science prospective teachers; and

(15) To find out the correlation between intelligence and personality of graduate and post-graduate prospective teachers.

The *normative survey method* was used. This method investigates into the conditions and relationships that exist at present in the context of intelligence and personality.

Variable is a condition or characteristic which the experimenter manipulates, controls or observes. For the present study the *variables* chosen were: (1) Gender (Male and Female Prospective Teachers); (2) Locality (Rural and Urban Prospective Teachers); (3) Teaching Methodology (Arts and Science Prospective Teachers); and (4) Educational Qualification (Graduate and Post-Graduate Prospective Teachers).

Hypotheses are guesses or tentative generalizations which provide basis to the whole study to be tested by facts. For the present study, the *hypotheses* framed were: (1) There is no very superior intelligence in prospective teachers; (2) There is no significant difference in the intelligence of male and female prospective teachers; (3) There is no significant difference in the intelligence of rural and urban prospective teachers; (4) There is no significant difference in the intelligence of prospective teachers of arts and science methodology; (5) There is no significant difference in the intelligence of graduate and post-graduate prospective teachers; (6) There is no emotionally well balanced personality in prospective teachers; (7) There is no significant difference in the personality of male and female prospective teachers; (8) There is no significant difference in the personality of rural and urban prospective teachers; (9) There is no significant difference in the personality of prospective teachers of arts and science methodology; (10) There is no significant difference in the personality of graduate and post-graduate prospective teachers; (11) There is no correlation between intelligence and personality of prospective teachers; (12) There is no correlation between intelligence and personality of male and female prospective teachers; (13) There is no correlation between intelligence and personality of rural and urban prospective teachers; (14) There is no correlation between intelligence and personality of prospective teachers of arts and science methodology; and (15) There is no correlation between intelligence and personality of graduate and post-graduate prospective teachers.

A *sample* is a small group which represents all the traits and characteristics of the population. The prospective teachers studying in Colleges of Education of Ranga Reddy district were selected as population. The *stratified random sampling* technique was used in selecting the sample. The sample size was 600 prospective teachers.

A research tool is a tool used for the purpose of data collection. The tools used in the present study were *The Group Test of General Mental Ability* standardized by S. Jalota and *Personality Inventory Scale* standardized by Eysenck.

For the analysis of the data, suitable statistical techniques like mean, standard deviation and critical ratio were used.

## CONCLUSIONS AND DISCUSSION

From the analysis of the data, the following conclusions are drawn and these are followed by necessary discussion:

1. **The prospective teachers are holding a bright average level of intelligence.**

The present state of intelligence, if we consider intelligence as a product of learning and as a function of interaction and if we set aside intelligence as genetic endowment, intelligence may be due to the nature of course work as the prospective teachers encounter totally new content as well as new practical experiences in teaching. This may also be due to the awareness that the mastery of subject matter of pedagogy helps in getting a teacher job through the test conducted by the government, for which the prospective teachers need to learn and work more when compared to their previous education.

The prospective teachers may enhance their intelligence by developing better study habits, by participating in all pedagogical activities intensively, by participating in yoga, meditation, etc., by developing achievement motivation and by enhancing academic achievement. Their intelligence can also be improved by mingling with co-students in performing different kinds of activities like Quiz competitions, debates, etc., as per the norms and standards laid down in the course work.

**2. The male and female prospective teachers have a bright average level of intelligence without any significant difference between them.**

This result is supporting the studies of Dei, S.L. (1991), Kumar, D. (1981), Ray, Mrinmarji (1988), Gupta Jyothika and Ram, Sukhjinder (2006) who reported no significant difference between boys and girls on intelligence.

The contradictory studies of Gupta, K.L. (1977) found a significant difference at 0.01 level in the intelligence of boys and girls, with boys having higher intelligence. Sahai, S.K. (1985) and Singh, K.K. (1985) reported that males were higher on mean intelligence as compared to females. Tripathi, R.C. (1986) investigated that girls had better average scores in intelligence.

The common course material provided, the common goals and aspirations of becoming a good teacher, the undifferentiated aim of getting a government job, the mental as well as physical maturity, surrounding environment, their attitudes etc., might have played a legitimate role in having no significant difference in the level of intelligence of male and female prospective teachers.

Both the male and female prospective teachers can enhance their intelligence by developing better skills of teaching and learning, by better audio-visual aids, by maintaining good relations with others and by inner motivation.

It must lead to innovations in various fields of knowledge which is an aptitude tract and must become a way of life. The individual has to avoid the usual routine conventional way of thinking and doing things and practice to produce a quantity of ideas, which are original, novel and which are workable.

3. **The rural and urban prospective teachers are holding a bright average level of intelligence with a significant difference between them. The urban prospective teachers are with more intelligence than their counter-parts.**

The mean intelligence score of urban prospective teachers was found to be more than the rural prospective teachers. This result is supporting the studies of Bhattacharya, Anjana (1989) and Tripathi, R.C. (1986), which stated that, the urban are more intelligent than the rural.

The contradictory study of Gupta, K.L. (1977) found that rural and urban location was not related to intelligence.

As the prospective teachers of rural and urban localities strive equally for better achievement in pedagogical activities, they should increase their intelligence by following the recent learning strategies in order to master the subject matter.

The teaching learning material used is to be according to the recent needs of the pupils and according to the recent technological developments taking place. The quality of instruction and community sense should be increased. The teacher's professional competency as those of knowledge, abilities and beliefs must be brought to the teaching situation.

4. **The prospective teachers of arts and science faculties are possessing a bright average level of intelligence with a significant difference between them. The science prospective teachers are holding more intelligence than arts prospective teachers.**

The mean intelligence of the science methodology prospective teachers is more as compared to the arts methodology prospective teachers. This result is supporting the studies of Chatterji, P.S. (1983) and Gupta, B.D. (1988) which stated that science teachers were more intelligent than the arts teachers.

The contradictory study of Sharma, K. (1981) found no significant difference between science and arts students with respect to verbal ability. A significant difference was found between science and arts students in GIT, numerical and non-verbal activity. Burwani, Rupa G. (1991) found no difference in the intelligence of science and arts group teachers.

Though the science and arts prospective teachers perceive and have a different kind of knowledge of general education and teacher education, both of them have similar level of course work in teacher education. They have to develop more intelligence and become good teachers.

They can enhance their intelligence by making the classroom teaching more effective according to the interests and capacities of the pupils. The specific abilities of the students should be recognized and accordingly they have to be motivated. Intelligence promotes group acceptance. Assertiveness denote acceptance. The more conscious, more tender minded and more related we are, the better we are accepted by others.

5. **The graduate and post-graduate prospective teachers are possessing a bright average level of intelligence with a significant difference between them. The post-graduate prospective teachers are with high intelligence than graduate prospective teachers.**

The mean intelligence of post-graduate prospective teachers was more as compared to the graduate prospective teachers.

The graduate and post-graduate prospective teachers differ significantly in knowledge, age and maturation. They have to strive more so that they can prove as the best teachers.

Their intelligence can be enhanced by conserving and promoting the rich Indian culture and civilization. The community sense should be developed in them. Spontaneous behavior has its place in an educational setting and some of the best teaching moments happen because of spontaneous behavior. At the same time, planned behavior is also beneficial to be flexible as well.

**6. The prospective teachers are holding a highly extrovert personality.**

The present status of personality may be due to the nature of course work as the prospective teachers encounter with a new content and practical experiences in teaching. This may be due to the profession which they enter into, i.e., the teaching profession which is considered as a noble profession. So they have to modify themselves so that they may be role models to their students.

The prospective teachers may enhance their personality by participating in yoga, meditation, by developing internal motivation, by following certain rules, norms and standards of living, by participating in curricular and co-curricular activities and by giving the live examples of great personalities. If teachers need to be extroverts, they should enjoy the company of others. A teacher needs to be compassionate and cooperative rather than suspicious and antagonistic.

**7. The male and female prospective teachers are holding a highly extrovert personality without any significant difference between them.**

This result is supporting the studies of Gowri, Prasad (2005), Rajashekar S. and Raja Vaiyapuri, P. (2008) and Subhalakshmi, Nandi (2002) stated no significant difference in the level of personality of male and female prospective teachers. The studies of Bhoj, A.N.T. (1992), Chandra, Sekhar (2003), Dagaur, B.S. (1988), Kumar, Anil P.M. and Ayishabhi T.C. (2008), Poulose, P.J. (1988), Madhava, Kale (2007), Sharma, C.S. (1986), Subramonian, G. and Muthaiah, N. (2009) and Venkata, Rao

(2004) also stated no significant difference in the level of personality of male and female students.

The contradictory studies of Kaur, Satwinderpal (2008) and Sharma, S.K. (1986) stated a significant difference in the level of personality of male and female prospective teachers. The studies of Arunima (1989), Babu, Sameer M. (2009), Chandresekhar, K. (2006), Gupta, K.L. (1977), Jayanthi, N.L.N. and Padmanabhan, T. (2008), Joshi, Renuka (1989), Karuna, Sharma and Sadhana, Mahajan (2001), Khatoon, J. (1988), Kumari, Shiv (1990), Krishna, K.P. (1973), Sahai, S.K. (1985), Sharma, K.L. (1978), Singh Tirath and Kaur, Parminder (2008), Suresh, K.J. and Joshith, V.P. (2008), Uchat, D.A. (1979), Vidhu, M. (1968) and Vijayalakshmi, G. and Lavanya P. (2006) also stated a significant difference in the level of personality of male and female students.

The mental and physical maturity, the surrounding environment, the attitudes and aspirations of becoming a good teacher, the common aim and goal of getting a government job and the common course material provided have played am important role in having no significant difference in the level of personality of male and female prospective teachers.

They can enhance their personality by better perceptions and being well adjusted in their life with the changing circumstances in the day to day life. They must be prepared physically, mentally and socially as strong individuals so that they may be as role-models to others. A teacher needs to create an environment of safety, trust and positive learning without crossing over the line to let students take advantage of his or her agreeable nature. It is a fine line at times.

8. **The rural and urban prospective teachers are having a highly extrovert personality with a significant difference between them. The urban prospective teachers are more extrovert than rural prospective teachers.**

This result is supporting the studies of Gupta, K.L. (1977), Jayanthi, N.L.N. and Padmanabhan, T. (2008), Khatoon, J.

(1988), Srivastava, R.K. (1988) and Subramonian, G. and Muthaiah, N. (2009) which stated a significant difference between the personality of rural and urban students. The mean score of urban prospective teachers was found to be more than the rural prospective teachers.

The contradictory studies of Gowri, Prasad (2005), Usha, P. and Sasi, Kumar (2007) stated no significant difference between the personality of rural and urban prospective teachers. The studies of Chandra, Sekhar (2003), Madhava, Kale (2007), Venkata, Rao (2004) and Vijayalakshmi, G. and Lavanya, P. (2006) also stated no significant difference between the personality of rural and urban students.

The rural and urban prospective teachers strive equally for attaining better personality so that they can attain mastery over the subject and establish themselves as unique personality in teaching by using all the recent technologies of teaching and learning the subject matter.

They can enhance their personality by designing social programmes for the attainment of distant goals so as to reduce the tensions and conflicts which prevail.

9. **The prospective teachers of arts and science faculties are possessing a highly extrovert personality with a significant difference between them. The science prospective teachers are more extroverts than arts prospective teachers.**

This result is supporting the studies of Gupta, B.D. (1988) and Uchat, D.A. (1979) which stated a significant difference in the personality of prospective teachers of arts and science faculties. The study of Burwani, Rupa G. (1991) also showed a significant difference in the personality of arts and science students. The mean score of science prospective teachers was found to be more than the arts prospective teachers.

The contradictory studies of Natarajan and Balan, K. (2003), Rajashekar, S. and Raja, Vaiyapuri P. (2008) and Raghu,

A. and Mahender, Reddy S. (2008) which stated no significant difference between the personality of arts and science prospective teachers. The study of Chatterji, P.S. (1983) also showed no significant difference between the personality of arts and science students.

Both the arts and science teachers have unique personality due to the knowledge which they gain, the course content delivered and the nature of the general education provided to them. They have to develop themselves as good personalized people so as to become a good teacher. Promoting a creative teacher personality as well as providing a wide range of experiences aims at helping the teacher towards a creative approach to his teaching.

They can enhance their personality by valuing the feelings of others, regenerating the energy so as to be identified as better persons in the society.

10. **The graduate and post-graduate prospective teachers are possessing a highly extrovert personality with a significant difference between them. The post-graduate prospective teachers are more extroverts than their counterparts.**

This result is supporting the study of Subramonian, G. and Muthaiah, N. (2009) which stated a significant difference between the personality of graduate and post-graduate students. The mean score of post-graduate prospective teachers was found to be more than the graduate prospective teachers.

The contradictory study of Raghu, A. and Mahendar Reddy S. (2008) no significant difference between the personality of graduate and post-graduate prospective teachers. The study of Bharathi, L. (1988) also showed no significant difference between the personality of graduate and post-graduate students.

The graduate and post graduate prospective teachers differ significantly in knowledge, age and maturity. They differ in their perceptions and abilities. The interests and motives have to be taken into consideration in order to prove themselves as better teachers.

They can be made to achieve more useful perceptions in order to have an adequate concept of the self. The guidance procedures, differentiated programmes of study, courses and learning experiences, individualized teaching and learning procedures and other educational measures have to be designed to achieve greater satisfaction of individual needs.

**11. The prospective teachers are holding a high positive correlation between intelligence and personality.**

This result is supporting the studies of Nabi, Ahmed and Abdul, Rahman (2003), Sharma, K.L. (1978), Shukla, P. (1973) and Singh, R.S. (1980) which stated a positive correlation between intelligence and personality of students.

The contradictory study of Mishra, G. Santwana (2007) showed a negative correlation between intelligence and personality of prospective teachers. The studies of Kauser (1982), Narula, K.S. (1979), Rao, D.G. (1965), Singh, K.K. (1985), Sridhar, Y.N. and Hamid, Reza Badiei (2007), Venkata, Rao (2004) and Vidhu, M. (1968) also stated no correlation between intelligence and personality of the students.

The present status of intelligence and personality may be due to the nature of the course material as the prospective teachers encounter totally new content as well as new practical experiences in teaching. They need to learn and work more as compared to their previous education since the mastery of pedagogy helps them in getting a government job.

It is evident that the effective and efficient functioning of any institute primarily depends on the quality and commitment of its human resources. The right attitude towards the profession, involvement in teaching, concern over the profession, aptitude towards teaching zeal and enthusiasm in his profession and mental health of the teacher are essential requisite conditions to prevail in a teacher who could definitely bring success in his teaching programme.

**12. The male and female prospective teachers possess a high positive correlation between intelligence and personality.**

This result is supporting the studies of Ramganesh, E. and Johnson, N. (2008) and Usha, P. and Sasi, Kumar (2007) which stated a positive correlation between intelligence and personality of male and female prospective teachers. The studies of Konwar, L.N. (1989), Ramesh, Mandalapu (2005), Ramesh, R. and Ponnambala, Thiagarajan A. (2005), Sharma Brajesh Kumar, Subramanian and Narayana (2006) also stated a positive correlation between intelligence and personality of males and females.

The contradictory study of Laxmidhar, Behera and Sushant, Kumar (2004) stated a negative correlation of intelligence and personality of male and female prospective teachers. The studies of John, Louis Manoharan and Christie, Doss (2007), Joshi, Renuka (1989), Pal, Anitha (1988) and Sharma Brajesh Kumar, Subramanian and Narayana (2006) also showed a negative correlation of intelligence and personality of males and females.

The common goals and aspirations of becoming a good teacher, the material, the physical, mental and the social states, environmental conditions, the interests and abilities of male and female prospective teachers make them to have a high positive correlation between intelligence and personality so that they may become role models to their future generation.

A continuous inter-play or exchange of ideas between the Teacher and the taught occupies a priori central role in the learning of an individual.

**13. The rural and urban prospective teachers possess a high positive correlation between intelligence and personality.**

This result is supporting the studies of Usha, P. and Sasi, Kumar (2007) and Venkata, Ramana (2007) which stated a positive correlation between intelligence and personality of rural and urban prospective teachers. The studies of Jyothi, Prathibha A. (2003), Konwar, L.N. (1989), Patel, S.S. (1982) and Ramesh, R. and Ponnambala, Thiagarajan A. (2005) also showed a positive correlation of intelligence and personality of rurals and urbans.

The contradictory study of Ramganesh, E. (2006) showed a negative correlation between intelligence and personality of rural and urban prospective teachers. The studies of Bhatt, D.B. (1990), Darsana, M. (2007), Fatima, Shaik (2005), Khiangte, Varparhi (1988) and Singh, B.K. (1984) also showed a negative correlation between intelligence and personality of rurals and urbans.

As the prospective teachers of rural and urban localities strive equally for better achievement in pedagogical activities, they have a high positive correlation between intelligence and personality. The personality development programmes, the programmes to enhance the intelligence, the self motivation, the mode of instruction and the mode of teaching learning material play a significant factor in the enhancement of intelligence and personality.

Teachers responsibility does not seize when he has satisfied the average individual in the class, though they are more in numbers. To quench the thirst of the gifted individual, the teacher should keep himself abreast with new techniques and novel strategy which is not an easy job and it is a hard task to successfully achieve. Still baffling problem for every ideal teacher is to go down to the level of the dullard and cater the needs of hard-to-reach individual in the class.

**14. The correlation between intelligence and personality in arts prospective teachers is moderately positive and it is highly positive correlation in science prospective teachers.**

This result is supporting the studies of Gupta, B.D. (1988) and Patil, Ajaykumar Bhimrao (2006) which stated a positive correlation between intelligence and personality of arts methodology and science methodology prospective teachers. The study of Jhag (1979) also showed a positive correlation between intelligence and personality of arts and science students.

The contradictory study of Laxmidhar, Behera and Sushant, Kumar (2004) showed a negative correlation between intelligence and personality of arts methodology and science methodology prospective teachers. The study of Arockiadoss, S. and Karumathur (2006) also stated a negative correlation between intelligence and personality of arts methodology and science methodology students.

Though the arts and science prospective teachers a different kind of knowledge on general and teacher education both of them have a high positive correlation between intelligence and personality. The audio-visual aids, the teaching learning material and the mode of instruction play a very important role in the development of intelligence and personality.

Teacher's role is pivotal in providing education and making the nation literature. To make the nation totally literate and to attain 'educational for all', to improve educational standards and to increase the level of achievement, the teacher should not only be committed and devoted but should also be competent and creative.

**15. The graduate and post-graduate prospective teachers possess a high positive correlation between intelligence and personality.**

This result is supporting the study of Ramganesh, E. (2006) which stated a positive correlation between intelligence and personality of graduate and post-graduate students.

The contradictory study of John, Louis Manoharan and Christie, Doss (2007) showed a negative correlation between intelligence and personality of graduate and post-graduate students.

Though the graduate and the post graduate teachers differ significantly in knowledge, age and maturity there is a good sign of having a highly positive correlation between intelligence and personality. A sort of community sense should be developed in them by making them to participate in different activities and by conserving and promoting the rich Indian culture and civilization to the future generations.

Education comprises of a positive science of learning and creative art of teaching. But in most, the formal teaching is neglected. Teachers always want a correct answer but not clever answer. Most of the teachers should avoid this and strive for excellence in teaching.

The prospective teachers studying in Colleges of Education are with a bright average level of intelligence and with a highly extrovert personality. Except gender, the locality, the methodology and the qualification of prospective teachers show an influence on the level of intelligence and personality of prospective teachers.

The prospective teachers, the teacher educators and the social and educational environment should make the prospective teachers feel comfortable during their course period. The prospective teachers should enhance their intelligence and personality by better strategies. Better skills, good relations with peers and teachers, good teaching learning material, audio-visual aids, good instruction, self motivation, academic achievement, adjustment, yoga and meditation, better study habits, good life skills, appropriate aspirations etc. will help the prospective teachers in enhancing their intelligence and personality. The prospective teachers should develop and improve all of the above in order to master the teacher education skills, knowledge and to become expert teachers in future after rolling out of the Colleges of Education.

## SUGGESTIONS FOR FUTHER RESEARCH

The present study, A Study of Intelligence and Personality of Prospective Teachers, brings to light a good number of new areas to be studied by future researchers. The areas and variables that are not covered by this study may be put to test to enlighten the other associated factors. So, the researchers may think of the following areas of study in detail.

1. This study can be extended to students of all secondary school classes, intermediate, graduation and post-graduation at district and state levels.
2. Studies can be taken up to know the effect of factors like age, stage of education, socio-economic status, attitude, adjustment, creativity and other factors on intelligence and personality.
3. Studies can be taken up to know the influence of intelligence and personality on the academic achievement.
4. Studies can be considered to know the impact of education, employment, economic status, etc., of parents on the intelligence and personality of children/students.
5. Studies can be undertaken to find out the influence of school environment, home environment, teachers and co-students on the intelligence and personality of students.
6. Studies can be conducted to know the intelligence and personality of the students of all adolescent levels at district and state level.

# Bibliography

Abraham, P.A. (1969). *An Experimental Study of Certain Personality Traits and Achievement of Secondary School Pupils.* Ph.D. Psychology, Kerala University.

Acharya, P. (1991). *Personality Correlates of Matching Figure Test: An Empirical Study.* M.Phil. Psychology, Utkal University.

Adaval, S. (1973). *A Study of Conformity Behaviour as Related to Anxiety and Other Personality Variables.* Ph.D. Psychology, Allahabad University.

Agarwal, R. (1985). *A Study of Feeling of Security in Morally Developed and Under-developed Adolescents as Related to Their Self-concept and Personality Pattern.* Ph.D. Psychology, Agra University.

Agarwal, Richa (1990). *The Interactive Effects of Goal-setting Behaviour, Risk Taking and Prolonged Deprivation on Learning Performance Among School-going Female Adolescents.* Ph.D. Psychology, Agra University.

Aggarwal, Vigya (1989). *Factors Related to the Quality of Working Life.* Ph.D. Psychology, Kurukshetra University.

Agociya, Devindra Pal (1992). *A Cross-sectional Study of Personality, Values and Altruistic Behaviour of Youth Workers.* Ph.D. Psychology, Punjab University.

Ahuja, Malvinder and Tachanut, Yaiuva (2006). *Effectiveness of Multimedia CAI and Conventional Learning Conditions in Relation to Persistence of Professional College Students.* University News, 44, (52), 13-21.

Ajwani, J.K. (1979). *Problem-solving Behaviour in Relation to Personality, Intelligence, Age and Sex*. Ph.D. Psychology, RSU.

Akthar, S.N. (1970). *Attitude Modifiability as a Function of Some Personality Factors.* Ph.D. Psychology, Bhagalpur University.

Alegaokar, P.M. (1981). *Effect of Physical Achievement on Intelligence.* Ph.D. Education, Poona University.

Amin, N. (1982). *A Study of Relationship Between Spatial Ego-centrism and Conservation of Length and Area in Delhi School Children.* Ph.D. Education, Jamia Millia Islamia University.

Anagha, Lavalekar (2001). *Intelligence and Awareness of Social Problems.* Journal of Psychological Research, 45, (1), 36-42.

Anantha, Lakshmi (2005). *A Study of Negative Thinking of Students at Plus 2 Level.* M.Ed. Dissertation, Acharya Nagarjuna University.

Anderson, C.C. and Cropley, A.J. (1966). *Some Correlates of Originality.* Australian Journal of Psychology, 18, 218-227.

Ansari, Md. F.B. (1974). *A Study of Flexibility-rigidity Personality Trait Among Indian Students.* Ph.D. Psychology. Agra University.

Arockiadoss, S. and Karumathur (2006). *Learner Effectiveness and Academic Performance of College Students.* Experiments in Education, 34, (7), 3-13.

Aruna, N.S. (1981). *A Study of the Factors Influencing the Achievement of Standard VII Students Belonging to SC and ST's Whose Medium of Instruction is Kannada.* Ph.D. Education, Mysore University.

Arunima (1989). *Aggression Among Children. A Socio-psychological Appraisal.* Ph.D. Psychology, Punjab University.

Asthana, Anju (1989). *A Study of Social Maturity Among School-going Children in the City of Lucknow.* Ph.D. Education, Lucknow University.

Asthana, Usha (1990). *Internal and External Conditions of Control as Determinants of Performance in Relation to Personality Characteristics and Individuals Locus Control.* Ph.D. Education, Lucknow University.

Aurora, S. (1980). *A Comparative Study of Personality Factors of Deviant and Non-deviant Higher Secondary School-going Boys.* Ph.D. Psychology, Agra University.

Babu, Sameer M. (2009). *Self-Experience in School and its Relationship with Social Science Achievement.* EduTracks, 8, (8), 41-43.

Bali, S.S. (1981). *A Study of Common Personality Factors of Highly Creative Persons in Different Fields.* Ph.D. Education, Kurukshetra University.

Bansibihari, Pandit (2004). *Emotional Intelligence of Secondary Teachers.* EduTracks, 4, (4), 23-25.

Bansibihari, Pandit and Lata, Surwade (2006). *The Effect of Emotional Maturity on Teacher Effectiveness.* EduTracks, 6, (1), 37-38.

Barlinge, M.K. (1977). *A Study of Influence of Mothers Personality on Childs Personality.* Ph.D. Psychology, Nagpur University.

Baruah, Mukul Kumar (1988). *Socio-psychological Characteristics of Professional and Non-professional Students.* Ph.D. Education, Dibrugarh University.

Batania, Kulwanth Singh (2007). *Attitudinal Study of Teachers Towards Orientation Scheme of UGC.* University News, 45, (39), 24-30.

Behera, Laxidhar (2004). *Performance of B.Ed. Trainees.* EduTracks, Annual Subscription, 34-36.

Best, John W. and James, V. Khan (2005). *Research in Education.* 9th Edition. New Delhi: Prentice Hall of India Private Limited.

Bhadury, J. (1989). *The Effect of Feedback in Improving Personality, Desirable Behaviours, Values and Teacher Perception Among Secondary and Senior Secondary School Students.* Ph.D. Psychology, Utkal University.

Bhagavathy, G.P.K. (1977). *Analytical Study of Personality, Intelligence, Values and Problems of Adolescent Girls.* Ph.D. Education, Kerala University.

Bharadwaj, R.L. (1978). *Vocational Interests and Functions of Creativity Components, Intelligence and Socio-economic Status Among College-going Students.* Ph.D. Psychology, Agra University.

Bharambe, M.D. and Pandit, K.L. (1991). *Attitudinal Change: An Experimental Study.* Indian Educational Review, 26 (3), 42-54.

Bharamble, M.D. (1991). *A Multivariate Analysis of Attitudinal Change in Children: An Experimental Study.* Ph.D. Education, Nagpur University.

Bharathi, K. (1988). *Casual Thinking in Indian Children.* Indian Educational Review, 23, (3), 63-82.

Bharathi, L. (1988). *Role-Conflict and Personality Types as Stressors of Educated Working Women.* M.Phil. Education, Bangalore University.

Bhargava, K. (1980). *Self-disclosure as Related to Academic Competence and Personality (with special reference to Neurotic and Schizophrenic Personalities).* Ph.D. Psychology, Agra University.

Bhasin, Rajendra (1968). *A Study of Disparity Between Self-concept of Students as Perceived by Teachers and Peers.* Unpublished M.Ed. Dissertation, Delhi University.

Bhatnagar, R.P. (1967). *A Study of Some of the Personality Variables as Predictors of Academic Achievement.* Ph.D. Education, Delhi University.

Bhatt, D.B. (1990). *A Comparative Study of Some Personality Traits of Problematic and Non-problematic School-going Children.* Ph.D. Psychology, South Gujarat University.

Bhatt, Sahdev (1986). *Self-disclosure and Obedience Tendency as Determinants of Students Perception of Science Teacher: A Cross-Cultural Study.* Ph.D. Education, Kamaun University.

Bhattacharya, Anjana (1989). *A Cross-sectional Study of Some Differential Aptitudes of Secondary School Students.* Ph.D. Education, Kalyant University.

Bhoj, A.N.T. (1992). *Pattern of Cerebral Dominance and its Relation to Handedness, Cognitive Style, Creativity and Personality.* M.Phil. Psychology, Bangalore University.

Bhushan, L.I. (1968). *Personality Factors and Leadership Preference.* Ph.D. Psychology, Bhagalpur University.

Bhushan, R. (1985). *Certain Psychological Correlates of Beliefs in Superstitions.* Ph.D. Psychology, Bhagalpur University.

Buch, M.B., Chief Editor (1978-1983). *Third Survey of Research in Education.* Baroda: CASE, M.S. University of Baroda.

Buch, M.B., Chief Editor (1983-1988). *Fourth Survey of Research in Education.* New Delhi: NCERT.

Buch, M.B., Chief Editor (1988-1992). *Fifth Survey of Research in Education.* New Delhi: NCERT.

Burwani, Rupa G. (1991). *An Enquiry into the Nature of Self-concept in the Area of Competence and Its Impact on Mental Health and Academic Achievement.* Ph.D. Education, Visva Bharati University.

Cacha, Frances B. (1976). *Figural Creativity, Personality and Peer Nomination of Pre-adolescents.* Gifted Child Quarterly, 20, (2), 187-195.

Chamundeswari, S. and Vasanthi, S. (2009). *Job Satisfaction and Occupational Commitment Among Teachers.* EduTracks, 8,(6), 29-31.

Chandrasekhar, K. (2006). *Some Demographic and Personal Correlates of the Perception of Student Teachers of DIET's About Aspects of Their Training.* Experiments in Education, 34, (9), 3-13.

Chandra Sekhar, P. (2003). *A Study of the Relationship Between Co-curricular Activities and Personality of Secondary School Students of East Godavari District.* M.Ed. Dissertation, Acharya Nagarjuna University.

Chatterji, P.S. (1983). *A Comparative Study of Personality, Intelligence and Achievement Motivation of Students in Different Academic Groups.* Ph.D. Education, Patna University.

Chaturvedi, R.D. (1988). *Personality Factors, Value Orientation and Age as Correlates of Value Orientation and Age as Correlated of Attitude Towards Social Change.* Ph.D. Psychology, Agra University.

Chaudhary, N. (1971). *The Relationship Between Achievement Motivation and Anxiety, Intelligence, Sex, Social Class and Vocational Aspiration.* Ph.D. Psychology, Punjab University.

Chauhan, S.S. (1984). *A Comparative Study of the Achievement Motivation of ST and SC's of Himachal Pradesh in Relation to Their Intelligence, Socio-economic Status.* Department of Education, Himachal Pradesh University.

Chhotray, M. (1991). *Coping Through Humour: An Exploratory Investigation.* M.Phil. Psychology, Utkal University.

Chinara, B.D. (1992). *Effect of Strategies for Inculcation of Democratic Values Among Adolescents in Relation to Introversion, Extroversion and Value-related Behaviour Types.* Ph.D. Education, Punjab University.

Chopra, Reeta and Gartia, Radhakanta (2009). *Accountability of Secondary School Teachers in Relation to Their Occupational Stress.* EduTracks, 8, (7), 41-43.

Dagaur, B.S. (1988). *Relationship Between Neuroticism, Anxiety and Creative Thinking in the Context of Extroversion, Psychoticism and Sex.* Indian Educational Review, 23, (2), 15-31.

Dalu, Vatibha (1992). *A Study of Personality, Values and Religious Attitudes of Urban and Rural Males and Females in the Purview of Socio-economic Status.* Ph.D. Psychology, Agra University.

Darsana, M. (2007). *Relationship Between Emotional Intelligence and Certain Achievement Facilitating Variables of Higher Secondary School Students.* EduTracks, 7, (4), 25-31.

Dei, S.L. (1991). *Interrelationship Between Non-verbal Measures of Cognition.* M.Phil. Psychology, Utkal University.

Desai, H.G. (1971). *Effects of Intelligence of Birth Order and Sex.* Department of Education, Saurashtra University.

Dhall, Taruna C. and Salni, Madhu (2008). *Academic Performance of Elementary School Children of Working and Non-working Mothers.* EduTracks, 7, (5), 41-43.

Dhillon, G.K. (1979). *A Comparative Study of Personality Characteristics, Adjustment and Motivational Level of Participant and Non-Participant Children of Secondary Schools in Physical Activities.* Ph.D. Education, Punjab University.

Discippio, William J. (1971). *Divergent Thinking: A Complex Function of Interaction Dimensions of Extroversion-Introversion and Neuroticism Stability.* British Journal of Psychology, 62, (4), 545-550.

Dixit, G. (1963). *A Developmental Study of Rorschah Response Pattern of Children Between Five Plus and Ten Plus.* Ph.D. Psychology, Allahabad University.

Dubey, P. (1980). *The Study of Effects of Frustration on Personality Development.* Ph.D. Psychology, Kuvempu University.

Dubey, R. (1984). *A Comparative Study of the Personality, Intelligence and Performance of Psychotics and Neurotics.* Ph.D. Psychology, Agra University.

Dubois, Alverson Stanley (1979). *Educational Psychology and Institutional Decisions.* Illinois: The Dorsey Press Homewood.

Dutt, N.K. (2003). *Psychological Foundations of Education.* New Delhi: Doaba House.

Dutt, N.K., Bountra, P. and Sabhrawal, V.K. (1973). *A Study of Creativity in Relation to Intelligence, Extroversion and Neuroticism.* Indian Educational Review—A Research Journal, 8, (2), 13-16.

Dutt, Sunil (1989). *The Effect of Problem-solving Strategies on the Problem-solving Ability in Science of High School Students in Relation to Anxiety Level, Cognitive Style and Intelligence.* Ph.D. Education, Punjab University.

Dutt, Sunil (2001). *Relationship Between Verbal Creativity and Problem-solving Ability in Mathematics of Tenth Grades at Different Levels of Cognitive Style.* The Educational Review, 107, (3), 8-10.

Fatima, Shaik (2005). *An Investigation into the Reasoning Ability of Secondary School Students.* M.Ed. Dissertation, Acharya Nagarjuna University.

Fernandez P. and Venkataraman, D. (2003). *Inter-correlation Among Creative Characteristics and Ego States.* The Educational Review, 46, (3), 12-14.

Gaikwad, J.M. (1988). *A Study of Personality Traits of Elementary School Children in Relation to Their Mothers Marital Adjustment and Child Rearing Practices.* Ph.D. Home Science, Nagpur University.

Garga, Satish Chandra (1951). *Memory Span in Children of 12+.* Unpublished Dissertation (M.Ed.), Allahabad University.

George, M. (1969). *Personality Patterns of College Students Specializing in Different Fields.* Ph.D. Psychology, Kerala University.

Gnanaguru, Selvaraj A. and Kumar, Suresh M. (2008). *Under-Achievement of B.Ed. Students in Relation to Their Home Environment and Attitude Towards Teaching.* EduTracks, 7, (12), 20-22.

Godbole, A.Y. (1988). *A Story-telling: A Way for Doing the Childs Personality.* Ph.D. Psychology, Poona University.

Gowri, Prasad P. (2005). *A Study of Stress on Secondary School Teacher's in Guntur District.* M.Ed. Dissertation, Acharya Nagarjuna University.

Gupta, Alka (1992). *A Study of Students Academic Satisfaction as Related to Their Personality Needs and Personal Values.* Ph.D. Education, Allahabad University.

Gupta, A.K. (1980). *A Factorial Study of Verbal and Non-creativity, Intelligence and Socio-economic Status.* Model Institute of Education and Research, Jammu.

Gupta, B.D. (1988). *Intelligence, Adjustment and Personality Needs of Effective Teachers in Science and Arts.* Ph.D. Education, Agra University.

Gupta, Jyothika and Sukhjinder Ram (2006). *Transactional Styles Among Perspective Teachers: The Role of Sex Difference and Emotional Intelligence.* EduTracks, 6, (2), 34-37.

Gupta, Krishna Kumari (1988). *The Creative Development of Secondary School Children in Relation to sex, Intelligence and Urban and Rural Background.* Ph.D. Education, Agra University.

Gupta, K.L. (1977). *Individual Differences in Value Pattern and Personality Type of the School-going Adolescents of Eastern Uttar Pradesh.* Ph.D. Education, Gorakhpur University.

Gupta, Sushma (1991). *A Study of Deprivation in Relation to Certain Cognitive and Non-cognitive Variables Among Adolescents.* Ph.D. Education, Jammu University.

Gupta, V.K. (1976). *Relationship of Age, Sex, Level of Intelligence and Personality Adjustment to Extreme Response Style.* Ph.D. Psychology, Agra University.

Halpin, W. Gerald, Payne David A. and Ellaitle Cha D. (1974). *In Search of Creative Personality Among the Gifted Groups.* Gifted Child Quarterly, 18, (1), 31-33.

Hemantha Kumar, A.G. (2003). *A Study of the Problems of Adolescent Girls Related to Social Isolation.* The Educational Review, 46, (3), 4-9.

Hussain, M.Q. (1963). *Personality Adjustment Factors Discrimination between Criminals and Normals During Adolescence.* Ph.D. Psychology, Annamalai University.

Iwata, O. Samen (1968). *Some Relationship of Creativity with Intelligence and Personality Variables.* Psycholigia: An International Journal of Psychology in the Orient, 11, (3-4), 211-220.

Jabbal, K.J. (1981). *A Study of Development of Mathematical Concepts in School-going Children*. Ph.D. Education, Gorakhpur University.

Jacob, Annie K. (2007). *Relationship between Creativity and Self Concept*. EduTracks, 7, (2), 25-30.

Jailkhani, Neerja (1988). *The Effect of an Enrichment Programme Upon the IQ Scores of Lower Class Children*. Indian Educational Review, 23, (2), 63-70.

Jain Jayanti, R. (1990). *A Study of the Self-concept of Adolescent Girls and Identification with Parent and Parental Substitutes as Contributing to Realization of Academic Goals*. Ph.D. Education, Nagpur University.

Jain, Neelima (1990). *Effect of Perceivers and Stimulus Persons Religion and Sex on Person Perception*. Ph.D. Psychology, Lucknow University.

Jain, Neera (1989). *Family Structure, Parental Behaviour and Self-Esteem in Male and Female Adolescents*. Ph.D. Psychology, Lucknow University.

Jain, R. (1974). *Inter-Modality Transfer and Its Personality Correlates*. Ph.D. Psychology, Allahabad University.

Jain, S. (1983). *Concept Formation as a Function of Verbal Intelligence and Achievement Motivation*. Ph.D. Education, Rajasthan University.

Jaluria, Reeta (1988). *Humour as a Process and a Product of Personality, Creativity and Frustration*. Ph.D. Education, Agra University.

Jantli, R.T. (1988). *Relationship Between Teacher Behaviour, Pupil Personality and Pupil Growth Outcome*. Ph.D. Education, Karnataka University.

Jayanthi, N.L.N. and Padmanabhan, T. (2008). *Test Anxiety of Higher Secondary Students*. EduTracks, 8, (2), 36-37.

Jhag, D.S. (1979). *A Study of Personality Correlates of Creative Children 15 Plus Studying Science Subjects*. Ph.D. Education, Bhopal University.

Jit, R. (1985). *The Contribution of Fluid and Crystallized Intelligence to the Verbal and Spatial Abilities of Right-handed Males and Females*. Ph.D. Psychology, Meerut University.

John, Louis Manoharan and Christie, Doss (2007). *Emotional Maturity of Post Graduate Students in Pondicherry Region*. Experiments in Education, 35, (8), 11-13.

Jogi, J.K. (1984). *The Effect of Response on Achievement at Different Levels with Reference to Intelligence and Taxonomic Categories through a Programme in Micro-economics.* Ph.D. Education, Himachal Pradesh University.

Johi, J.K. (1984). *A Study of Ego-Identity and Values of Adolescents Living in Hill Areas of Kamaun Region in Relation to Their School and Home Environment*. Ph.D. Education, Kuvempu University.

Johnson, S.J. (1982). *Personality Characteristics of Sports Participants in High Schools.* Ph.D. Psychology, Kerala University.

Joshi, Renuka (1989). *A Study of Creativity in Relation to Personality, Locus of Control and Alienation*. Ph.D. Psychology, Punjab University.

Jyothi Prathibha, Allapati (2003). *A Study of the Independent Problem-solving Ability of Secondary School Students in Mathematics.* M.Ed. Dissertation, Acharya Nagarjuna University.

Kabu, C.L. (1980). *A Psychological Analysis of the Mathematically Gifted at the Secondary and Higher Levels of Education*. Ph.D. Education, Jammu University.

Kalpana, Mallela (2003). *A Study of the Parental Encouragement on the Academic Career of Intermediate Students.* M.Ed. Dissertation, Acharya Nagarjuna University.

Kar, S.B. (1961). *The Intelligence of the Homogeneous.* The Bihar Tribal Research Institute.

Karuna, Sharma and Sadhana, Mahajan (2001). *Gender Differences in Stress as Affected by Personality in Bank Employees.* Journal of Psychological Research, 45, (2), 78-83.

Karunanidhi, S. and Kaliappan, K.V. (1997). *Psychological Determinants of Writers Cramp.* Journal of Psychological Research, 41, (3), 134-139.

Kaur, Satwinderpal (2008). *Occupational Stress in Relation to Teacher Effectiveness Among Secondary School Teachers.* EduTracks, 7, (10), 27-29.

Kaur, Surinder Jit and Kaur, Harjit (2006). *Teacher's Efforts to Promote Emotional Intelligence among Adolescent Students.* University News, 44, (39), 7-10.

Kauser, F. (1982). *Children's Curiosity and Its Relationship to Intelligence, Creativity and Personality.* Ph.D. Psychology, Madras University.

Khatoon, J. (1988). *Personality Patterns of High and Low Academic Achievers: A Psychological Study of Adolescents of Rohilkhand Region, Uttar Pradesh.* Ph.D. Psychology, Rohilkhand University.

Khan, Saheel Md. and Srivastava Bina (2008). *Teacher-Burnout in Relation to Mental Health.* EduTracks, 7, (9), 31-33.

Khiangte, Varparhi (1988). *Non-cognitive Correlates of Creativity Among the Secondary School Students.* Ph.D. Education, North-Eastern Hill University.

Kohli, Om Prakash (1989). *A Study of Attitude of Students Towards Religion in Relation to Personality Characteristics, Intelligence and Socio-economic Status.* Ph.D. Education, Punjab University.

Komarik, E. (1972). *Creativity and Orthogonal Factors of Personality.* Sbornik Praci-Filosofici, Fakulty Brenske University, 20, (17), 115-124.

Konwar, L.N. (1989). *A Study of Socialization Practices at Home and School and Development of Personal Achievement Motivation Among Secondary School Pupils in Assam.* Ph.D. Education, Dibrugarh University.

Koteswara, M.N. and Ramachandra Reddy, B. (2001). *Impact of 14 Personality Factors on Reading Achievement of High School Students.* The Educational Review, 44, (10), 4-7.

Krishna, K.P. (1973). *A Study of Some Antecedents and Personality Correlates of Risk-taking Behaviour.* Ph.D. Psychology, Mag. University.

Kubie, L.S. (1958). *Neurotic Distortion of the Creative Provess.* Laurence Kansos Press.

Kumar (2001). *Abnormal Psychology.* Second Edition. Agra: Lakshmi Narain Agarwal.

Kumar, Anil P.M. and Ayishabhi, T.C. (2008). *Students Awareness of Values in the Content of Secondary Level English.* EduTracks, 7, (8), 30-31.

Kumar, D. (1981). *A Psychological Study of Intelligence and Intellectual Stimulation Received by the Students studying in Different Types of Junior High Schools of Tarai Area (Nainital) of UP.* Ph.D. Psychology, Kum. University.

Kumar, J. (1984). *The Effects of Extroversion and Elaboration of Encoding on Retrieval of Information.* Ph.D. Psychology, Meerut University.

Kumar Pramod, N. (2004). *A Study of Intelligence of the Students of Juvenile School and Government School.* M.Ed. Dissertation, Acharya Nagarjuna University.

Kumar, R.B. (1954). *Personality Traits of Indian Adolescent Girls, A Psycho Analytic Study.* Ph.D. Psychology, Allahabad University.

Kumari, Darshana (1986). *Intellectual Commitment and Educational Interest in Relation to Certain Cognitive and Non-cognitive Variables.* Ph.D. Education, Jammu University.

Kumari, Indira (1990). *A Study of Development of Logical Thinking in Pre-adolescents.* Ph.D. Education, Maharshi Dayanand University.

Kumari, Indira and Dagaur, B.S. (1992). *Piagetian Concepts of Conservation, Seriation and Classification in Relation to Intelligence.* Indian Educational Review, 27, (4), 73-85.

Kumari, Shiv (1990). *A Study of Modernity of Undergraduate Students with Respect to their Socio-economic Status, Self-concept and Level of Aspiration.* Ph.D. Education, Agra University.

Kumari, Sushma (1990). *A Study of Personality Characteristics, Intelligence, Achievement Motivation, Adjustment and Socio-economic Status of Juvenile and Adult Female Offenders.* Ph.D. Education, Agra University.

Kundu, C.L. (1989). *Personality Development.* New Delhi: Sterling Publishers Pvt. Limited.

Kuppuswamy, B. (2003). *Advanced Educational Psychology.* New Delhi: Sterling Publishers Private Limited.

Kurtzman, Kennith A. (1967). *A Study of School Attitudes, Peer Acceptance and Personality of Creative Adolescents.* Exceptional Children, 34, (3), 157-162.

Lakshmi, Rupa and Ran, Bijay Narayan Sinha (1996). *Personality Traits among Depressed Children.* Journal of Psychological Research, 40, (3), 107-110.

Latha (2001). *Type A and Hardiness. An Analysis of Its Components.* Journal of Psychological Research, 45, (1), 50-54.

Laxmi, Vibha and Chandel, N.P.S. (2008). *The Relationship Between Non-verbal Classroom Communication and Teaching Effectiveness.* EduTracks, 7, (5), 32-35.

Laxmidhar, Behera and Sushant, Kumar Roul (2004). *Performance of B.Ed. Trainees in Relation to Their Gender, Academic Background and Type of Institution.* The Educational Review, 47, (11), 6-11.

Leela, A.V.S. (1988). *Religiosity in Relation to Certain Personality Traits of College Students.* Ph.D. Psychology, Sri Venkateswara University.

Liebert, Obert M. and John, M. Neale (1977). *Psychology.* USA: John Wiley and Sons, Inc.

Madosh, A.G. (1989). *Personality Correlates of Sociometric Status: A Study of Sub-cultural Group Differences.* Indian Educational Review, 24, (1), 1-16.

Madhumathi, C. (1988). *Identification of Personality Correlates of Crime Prone Behaviour.* Ph.D. Education, Osmania University.

Madhava, Kale (2007). *A Study of Personality of Adolescent Students.* M.Ed. Dissertation, Acharya Nagarjuna University.

Magotra, H.P. (1982). *Mental Health as a Correlate of Intelligence, Education, Academic Achievement and Socio-economic Status.* Ph.D. Education, Jammu University.

Malhotra, D.K. (1975). *An Experimental Study of Problem-solving Behaviour as a Function of Personality, Drive and Practice.* Ph.D. Education, Pan. University.

Mangal, S.K. (1987). *Abnormal Psychology.* New Delhi: Sterling Publishers Private Limited.

Manoj, Kumar Dash (2005). *Assessment of Decision Making Ability: An Aspect of Quality Improvement.* EduTracks, 5, (4), 39-40.

Manoranjan, Panda (2005). *Correlation Between Academic Achievement and Intelligence of Class IX Students.* EduTracks, 5, (1), 36-38.

Mian, Shamshada (1988). *Intelligence, Neuroticism, Scholastic Achievement and Need Achievement: A Comparative Study Between Boys and Girls.* Ph.D., Education, Kashmir University.

Mishra, Brundaban, C.H. and Patel, Bananli (1990). *Students Liking Towards Their Teachers: Effect of Teacher Behaviour Feedback.* Indian Educational Review, 25, (12), 86-90.

Misra, K.N. (1991). *Inter-Relationship Between Organizational Conflict in School Teachers Stress and Burnout in Relation to Teachers Personality at Primary Level.* Ph.D. Education, Utkal University.

Muddu, V. (1980). *A Study of Some Personality Correlates of Intelligence and Creative Abilities Among High School Students in AP.* Ph.D. Education, Osmania University.

Murthy, Venkatesha C.G. and Rao, T.R. (1987). *A Study of the Effect of Japa Yoga on reactions to Frustration and Personality Dimensions.* The Mind, 14, (1), 23-31.

Murthy, Venkatesha C.G. (1988). *A Comparative Study of Juvenile Delinquents and Non-delinquents in Relation to Their Intelligence Level, Reactions to Frustrations, Family Size and Education.* The Mind, 14, (1), 7-15.

Nabi, Ahmed and Abdul, Rahman (2003). *Intelligence, SES and Adjustment as Correlates of Academic Achievement.* The Educational Review, 46, (9), 6-9.

Naik, Ramesh H. (2006). *Effect of Teachers Personality, Attitude and Teaching Effectiveness Rating on Students Academic Achievement.* Experiments In Education, 34, (4), 4-10.

Nanda, S.K. (2003). *Methodology of Educational Research and Educational Statistics.* New Delhi: Doaba Private House.

Narula, K.S. (1979). *A Study of Achievement Motivation, Personal Preferences, Perception, Anxiety, Risk-taking Behaviour and Other Correlates in Relation to Intelligence, Socio-economic Status and Performance of the Prospective Secondary School Teachers of Orissa State.* Ph.D. Education, MSU.

Natarajan, R. and Balan, K. (2003). *Performance of Arts-based Teachers and Science Based Teachers of Primary Schools.* The Educational Review, 46, (2), 18-19.

Ojha, R.K. (1962). *Intelligence and Intellectual Stimulation During Adolescence.* Ph.D. Psychology, AMU.

Pal, Anita (1988). *A Study of Competition and Co-operation in High School Children as Related to Personality and Parental Education.* Ph.D. Psychology, Punjab University.

Pal, Yesh (1992). *Inter-domain Relationship Between Intelligence and Personality and between Creativity and Personality by Canonical Analysis: Independent Study.* Indian Educational Review, 27, (4), 12-30.

Panda, S. (1991). *Effects of Certain Organismic Variables on Cognitive Style Among Pre-school Children and an Analysis of Its Correlates.* Ph.D. Home Science, Utkal University.

Pandey, Asha (2004). *Cognitive Competencies in Geography of Secondary Level Pupils of CBSE Schools in Uttar Pradesh.* Experiments in Education, 32, (8), 15-17.

Pandey, Sarala and Deb, Rakhi (2008). *Professional Attitude of Married and Unmarried Women Teachers of Higher Secondary Schools.* EduTracks, 8, (3), 38-41.

Paramesh, C.R. (1972). *Creativity and Personality.* First Edition, Janatha Book House, Madras-600014, India.

Pareek, A. (1984). *A Study of the Problematic Behaviour of Adolescents with Special Reference to Their Self and Other Acceptance and Attitude Towards Freedom.* Ph.D. Psychology, Agra University.

Pareek, D.L. (1990). *A Comparative Study of the Self-concept, Personality Traits and Aspirations of the Adolescents studying in Central Schools, State Government Schools and Private Schools in Rajasthan.* Ph.D. Education, Rajasthan University.

Patel, Kamla (1976). *Profiles of Creative Personality.* Psychologia: An International Journal of Psychology in the Orient, 19, (4), 173-183.

Patel, S. (1983). *Relation of Diet and Growth to Intellectual Growth among School Children in Orissa.* Department of Anthropology, Govt. College, Phulbani, Orissa. NCERT Financed.

Patel, S.S. (1982). *An Investigation into the Role of General Ability of Pre Primary School Children in relation to Reading Readiness.* Ph.D. Education, SPU.

Pathak, A.N. (1989). *Creativity and Personality.* New Delhi: Amar Prakashan Publishers.

Patil, Ajaykimar Bhimrao (2006). *Emotional Intelligence Among Student Teachers in Relation to Sex, Faculty and Academic Achievement.* EduTracks, 5, (7), 38-39.

Patil, I. (1982). *A Psychological Study of Intellectually Superiors.* Ph.D. Psychology, Karnataka University.

Phillips, Victor K. (1973). *Creativity: Performance, Profiles and Perceptions.* Journal of Psychology, 83, 25-30.

Pillai, K.S. (1981). *Sex Differences in certain Personality and Aptitude Dimensions-related to Science Achievement.* Ph.D. Education, Calicut University.

Poulose, P.J. (1988). *The Influence of Certain Personality Variables, Sex and Residence on Process Outcomes in Physics of University Entrants.* Ph.D. Education, Kerala University.

Pradhan, Renuka (1990). *Interpersonal Attraction Among Adolescent Boys and Girls Towards Each Other in Relation to Personality Make-up.* Ph.D. Psychology, Agra University.

Prakash, V. (1986). *A Study of Relationship Between Intelligence, Scholastic Achievement, Personality Traits and Achievement in Sports at Different Levels of Socio-economic Status.* Ph.D Physical Education, Kurukshetra University.

Pramod, Ku Prusty (2001). *Relationship Between Intelligence and Creativity.* The Educational Review, 44, (6), 7-9.

Purohit, Surabhi (2008). *Role of Parental Styles in Nurturing the Self-concept Among Adolescent Girls.* EduTracks, 7, (6), 34-37.

Qureshi, A.N. (1980). *A Study of Creativity in Relation to Intelligence, Manifest Anxiety and Level of Aspiration of High School Girls.* Ph.D. Psychology, Agra University.

Raghu, A. and Mahender Reddy, S. (2008). *Attitude of Student Teachers Towards Micro-teaching.* EduTracks, 7, (11), 27-31.

Rai, N.K. (1988). *A Comparative Study of Personality Dynamics of Blind Sighted Higher Secondary Students.* Ph.D. Education, Garh. University.

Raina, M.K. and Vats, Arunima (1989). *Occupational Difference and Type A Personality.* Indian Educational Review, 24, (1), 126-132.

Rajaram, V. (1995). *Personality Correlates of Decision Making Style.* Journal of Psychological Research, 39, (3), 47-52.

Rajashekar, S. and Raja Vaiyapuri, P. (2008). *Higher Secondary Teachers' Computer Anxiety.* EduTracks, 7, (8), 39-40.

Ramesh, Mandalapu (2005). *A Study of Mathematical Problem Solving Ability of IX Class Students in Prakasam District.* M.Ed. Dissertation, Acharya Nagarjuna University.

Ramesh, R. and Ponnambala Thiagarajan, A. (2005). *Self Concept of B.Ed. Trainees.* EduTracks, 4, (10), 33-34.

Ramganesh, E. (2006). *Emotional Maturity of Teacher Trainees.* Experiments In Education, 34, (4), 11-15.

Ramganesh, E. and Johnson, N. (2008). *Emotional Quotient of Teacher Educators.* EduTracks, 7, (9), 34-37.

Ramiah, L. (1990). *A Relational Study of Parent Involvement and Self Concept of Standard IX Students in Devakottai Educational District.* M.Phil. Education, Alagappa University.

Rani, R. (1986). *Intellectual and Non-intellectual Correlates of Creative Female School Students.* Ph.D. Psychology, Mag. University.

Rao, D.G. (1965). *A Study of Some Factors Related to Scholastic Achievement.* Ph.D. Education, Delhi University.

Rao, N.C.S. (1951). *Strategy in Concept Learning.* Allahabad Indian International Publications, 95-96.

Ray, Mrinmarji (1988). *Ethnic difference in Intelligence.* Indian Educational Review, 23, (2), 114-119.

Reddy, Y. Sudhakara and D. Bhaskara Rao (2003). *Creativity in Adolescents.* New Delhi: Discovery Publishing House.

Sahai, S.K. (1985). *A Study of Relationship of Students Sex Role Identity with Intelligence and Certain Personality and Demographic Variables.* Ph.D. Psychology, Punjab University.

Sambhi, Punam (1989). *A Study of the Value Patterns and Some Personality Variables of the Students studying in Three Institutions—Sri Satya Sai High School, Higher Secondary School, Missionary School and Central School in Andhra Pradesh.* Ph.D. Education, Himachal Pradesh University.

Samuel, Premela (1988). *Personality, Socialisation and Moral Development of High School Students.* Ph.D. Education, Poona University.

Sandhu, Sadhana (1990). *Construction of Triguna Personality Scale and Its relationship to Eysenck's Personality Model.* Ph.D. Psychology, Punjab University.

Santosh and Kaur, Ravdeep (2009). *Socio-economic Status as a Correlate of Vocational Interests of Secondary School Students.* EduTracks, 8, (6), 35-38.

Santwana G. Mishra (2007). *Teaching Attitude Score: A Criterion for Admission in College of Education.* EduTracks, 6, (6), 25-27.

Saulade, S.D. (1989). *Verbal Maze Learning: It's Cognitive and Personality Determinants.* Ph.D. Psychology, Nagpur University.

Saxena, P.C. (1981). *A Study of Interests, Need Patterns and Adjustment Problems of Over and Under Achievement.* Model Institute of Education and Research, Jammu.

Selvaraj A., Nellaiyappam N.O., Muthumanickam R. and Suresh, Kumar M. (2005). *Perception of Guide Teachers About Guiding B.Ed. Trainees.* Experiments in Education, 33, (3), 16-18.

Selwyn, S. and Ben, Sam W. (2004). *Self Concept, Intelligence and Attitude Towards Teaching of D.T.Ed. Students.* Experiments in Education, 32, (9), 10-13.

Sen, Gupta M. (1979). *Intellective and Non-intellective Factors Associated with Engineering Creativity.* Ph.D. Education, Meerut University.

Shah, Suhasini H. (1992). *A Study of the Effectiveness of Educational Programmes for Developing Skills of Thinking.* Ph.D. Education, Saurashtra University.

Shahin, A. (1971). *A Study of Intellecutal Abilities and Psycho-social Motor Behaviour among Pre School Children.* Ph.D. Psychology, Agra University.

Sharma, Anita (2008). *Commitment Among Teachers with Regard to Some of Their Personal and Academic Variables.* EduTracks, 8, (1), 42-44.

Sharma, Archana (1989). *An Experimental Study of Psychomotor Performance and Reminiscence as Determined by Personality, Intelligence, Sex and Practice.* Ph.D. Psychology, Punjab University.

Sharma, Brajesh Kumar and Patnaik, Sabita Prava. (2009). *Organizational Health of Elementary Schools and Job Satisfaction of Teachers.* EduTracks, 8, (6), 32-34.

Sharma, Brajesh Kumar, Subramanian K.B. and Narayana U.L. (2006). *Relationship Between Self Concept, Academic Motivation and Achievement in Mathematics: A Gender Comparison.* EduTracks, 5, (9), 29-32.

Sharma, C.S. (1986). *Personality Characteristics Contributing to Leadership Effectiveness.* Ph.D. Education, Meerut University.

Sharma, K. (1981). *Some Socio-economic Characteristics and Intellectual Abilities of High School Students.* Ph.D. Psychology, Mag. University.

Sharma, K.G. (1972). *A Comparative Study of Adjustment of Over and Under Achiever.* Ph.D. Education, Aligarh Muslim University.

Sharma, K.L. (1978). *A Comparative Study of Self Concept of High and Low Achievement of Intelligence Group of Students of Class Tenth in Urban Schools of Bareilly.* Ph.D. Education, Agra University.

Sharma, M. (1980). *A Study of Satisfaction and Dissatisfaction with School Among Adolescent Boys in Relation to their Personality Characteristics, Intelligence, Scholastic Performance and SES.* Ph.D. Education, Punjab University.

Sharma, Mala and Sharma, Suman. (2009). *Attitude of Science Teachers Towards Project Method.* EduTracks, 8, (6), 40-43.

Sharma, N.K. (1981). *A Comparative Study of Extroversion, Neuroticism, Achievement Motivation and Adjustment of Tribal, Rural and Urban Youth of Himachal Pradesh.* Ph.D. Psychology, Panjab University.

Sharma, R.K. (1978). *An Analysis of Factors Influencing the Behaviour Patterns of Adolescents Studying in Different School Environments.* Ph.D. Education, Punjab University.

Sharma, S.K. (1986). *Values of College Students of Different Socio-Economic Groups and relationship with their Intelligence and Adjustment in the Colleges.* Ph.D. Education, M.Sukh. University.

Shukla, P. (1973). *Development of Psychological Space Perception in Children.* Ph.D. Psychology, Allahabad University.

Sinha, D.N. (1966). *A Psychological Analysis of Some Factors Associated with Success and Failure in University Education: A Summary of the Findings.* Indian Educational Review, 13, (2), 34-47.

Sinha, N.C.P. and Sharma, M. (1978). *Creativity and Adjustment.* Indian Psychological Review, 16, (2), 4-7.

Singh, B.K. (1980). *Personality Factors of the Parents as Related to the Sex Role Preferences of the Children.* Ph.D. Psychology, Jodhpur University.

Singh, B.K. (1984). *A Psychological Study of the Patterns of Personality Variables of Rural and Urban College Students of Agra Region.* Ph.D. Psychology, Agra University.

Singh, E.L. (1979). *Superstitiousness: Its Personality Correlates Among the College Teachers.* Ph.D. Psychology, Nagpur University.

Singh, K.K. (1985). *Some Personality Factors of High and Low Intelligent Boys and Girls of Bhagalpur.* Ph.D. Psychology, Bhagalpur University.

Singh, O.P. (1982). *A Study of Creativity in High School Students in Relation to Intelligence and SES.* Ph.D. Education, Avadh University.

Singh, R.S. (1980). *Personality Variables (Traits and Needs) and Demographic Correlates (Sex, Area and SES) of Anxiety Level among College Students.* Ph.D. Psychology, Agra University.

Singh, Tirath and Kaur, Parminder. (2008). *Effect of Meditation on Self Confidence of Student Teachers in Relation to Gender and Religion.* EduTracks, 7,(11), 32-36.

Singh, Y. (1978). *An Examination of Personality Assessment of Mentally Superior and Average Children.* Department of Psychology, ST.John's College, Agra.

Singhaulakh, S.P. (1979). *Student Motivation to Work.* Ph.D. Education, Rajasthan University.

Sinha, J.K.P. (1986). *A Study of Personality Disposition and Achievement Motivation of Prejudiced College Students.* Ph.D. Psychology, Mag. University.

Sr. Eve, Justina Remould (2006). *Enhancing Emotional Intelligence of Student Teachers through Enneagram Educational Programme.* EduTracks, 6, (3), 25-31.

Sridhar, Y.N. and Hamid, Raza Badiei (2007). *Teacher Efficacy and Emotional Intelligence of Primary School Teachers.* EduTracks, 7, (3), 25-31.

Srinivas, Kumar D. (2002). *Temperamental Traits of Popular Teachers.* The Educational Review, May 2002, 88-92.

Srivastava, B. (1982). *A Study of Creativity in Relation to Personality Factors, Birth Order and Linguistic Ability Among the High School Students.* Ph.D. Education, Avadh University.

Srivastava, P. (1981). *A Comparative Study of Radicalism* vs. *Conservatism Traits Among Adolescent Boys and Girls of Intermediate Colleges of Lucknow.* Ph.D. Education, Avadh University.

Srivastava, R.K. (1988). *Personality Needs associated with Locality and Sex Variables.* Indian Educational Review, 23, (3), 151-155.

Srivastava, R.K. and Saxen, V. (1979). *Personality Correlates of Self-rated Academic Success and Failure: A Comparative Study.* Project Financed by P.P.N. College, Kanpur.

Subhalakshmi, Nandi (2002). *Organizational Stress Characteristics of Bengali Medium Secondary School Teachers.* The Educational Review, 45, (5), 17-19.

Subhashini, Y. (2005). *Impact of Peace Education on Emotional Balance in Secondary School Students.* M.Ed. Dissertation, Acharya Nagarjuna University.

Subramonian, G. and Muthaiah, N. (2009). *Perception of Students towards Total Quality Management (TQM) in Teacher Education Institutions, Coimbatore.* EduTracks, 8, (6), 34-38.

Sultana, M. (1983). *Intelligence, Social Competence and Parental Attitude in Normal and Deviant Children.* Ph.D. Psychology, Agra University.

Suneetha, Sannidhi (2007). *Problem-solving Ability in Physical Science of X Class Students: A Study.* M.Ed. Dissertation, Acharya Nagarjuna University.

Sunil Kiran, K.S. (2005). *A Study of the Impact of Emotional Intelligence on Academic Achievement of Junior College Students.* M.Ed. Dissertation, Acharya Nagarjuna University.

Suresh, K.J. and Joshith, V.P. (2008). *Emotional Intelligence as a Correlate of Stress of Student Teachers.* EduTracks, 7, (12), 26-32.

Suri, Ishwar Saran (1989). *An Investigation into the Structure of Reasoning Ability of the 15 year Old Students Belonging to Rural and Urban Areas.* Ph.D. Education, Jamia Millia Islamia University.

Swami, Priyankant M. (1989). *A Study of the Adjustment, Anxiety, Self-concept and Intelligence of Orphan Students Living in Orphanages as Compared to Normal Students.* Ph.D. Education, Saurashtra University.

Tiwari, Govind and Roma, Pal (1984). *Abnormal Psychology—Dynamic Approach.* Agra: Vinod Pustak Mandir.

Tiwari, Rajesh Kumar (1997). *Personality Correlates of Smoking.* Journal of Psychological Research, 41, (1 & 2), 1-4.

Tripathi, R.C. (1986). *Motivation and Its Correlates of High School Students of East Uttar Pradesh.* Ph.D. Education, Gorakhpur University.

Tripathy, A.N. (1986). *Home and Personality Determinants of Intelligence and Social Competency of Tribal and Non-tribal Children.* Ph.D. Psychology, Utkal University.

Uchat, D.A. (1979). *Study of the Self-concept of Pre-university Students Enrolled in the Arts, Science and Commerce Faculties of Saurashtra University.* Ph.D. Education, Saurashtra University.

Usha, P. and Sasi, Kumar P. (2007). *Teacher Commitment and Teachers Self-Concept as Predictors of Job Satisfaction.* EduTracks, 6, (12), 26-29.

Vasanthi, A. (2008). *Impact of Decision-making Style on Morale of the Teachers.* EduTracks, 8, (4), 32-35.

Venkata, Ramana, R. (2007). *An Analytical Study of the Professional Competence Among Secondary School Teachers.* M.Ed. Dissertation, Acharya Nagarjuna University.

Venkata Rao, B. (2004). *A Comparative Study of the Personality Characteristics of High and Low Academic Achievers.* M.Ed. Dissertation, Acharya Nagarjuna University.

Verma, B.P. (1990). *Sex-related Differences in Risk-Taking, Self Confidence and Anxiety Among Adolescent Learners.* Indian Educational Review, 25, (4), 93-97.

Vidhu, M. (1968). *The Relationship Between Neuroticism and Extroversion to Intelligence and Educational Achievement at Different Age Levels.* Ph.D. Psychology, Punjab University.

Vijayalakshmi, G. (2002). *Teachers Perception of School Children's Values.* EduTracks, 2, (4), 22-24.

Vijayalakshmi, G. and Lavanya, P. (2006). *Relationship Between Stress and Mathematics Achievement Among Intermediate Students.* EduTracks, 5, (11), 34-37.

Vijayalakshmi, R. (1991). *Relationship Between Self-concept and Personality Adjustment of Family Reared and Institution Reared Children.* M.Phil. Education, Madurai Kamaraj University.

Walberg, H.J. and Welch, W.W. (1967). *Personality Characteristics of Innovative Physical Teachers.* Journal of Creative Behaviour, 1, 169-171.

Yadav, R.S. (1991). *Factors Affecting Intelligence.* Indian Educational Review, 26, (1), 95-106.

Zahir, Saida. (1988). *A Study of Relationship Between Perceived Maternal Behaviour and Personality as well as Scholastic Achievement of Adolescents.* Ph.D. Education, Lucknow University.

Zargar, A.H. (1980). *A Study of Expression, Neuroticism and n-Achievement in Relation to Intelligence, Creativity and Scholastic Achievement.* Ph.D. Education, Kashmir University.

**Additional Reading**

Appala Naidu, P.Ch., Author and Digumarti Bhaskara Rao, Editor (2007). *Student Feedback Methods.* New Delhi : Discovery Publishing House.

Bhaskara Rao, Digumarti (1994). *Scientific Aptitude.* New Delhi : Ashish Publishing House. ISBN 81-7024-658-X.

Bhaskara Rao, Digumarti (1995). *Animal Kingdom.* New Delhi : Discovery Publishing House. ISBN 81-7141-274-2.

Bhaskara Rao, Digumarti (1995). *Batracology.* New Delhi : Discovery Publishing House. ISBN 81-7141-279-3.

Bhaskara Rao, Digumarti (1997). *Scientific Attitude.* New Delhi : Discovery Publishing House. ISBN 81-7141-381-1.

Bhaskara Rao, Digumarti (1996). *Scientific Attitude vis-à-vis Scientific Aptitude.* New Delhi : Discovery Publishing House. ISBN 81-7141-308-0.

Bhaskara Rao, Digumarti (2004). *Scientific Attitude, Scientific Aptitude and Achievement.* New Delhi : Discovery Publishing House. ISBN 81-7141-781-7.

Bhaskara Rao, Digumarti (2004). *Educational Administration.* New Delhi : Discovery Publishing House. ISBN 81-7141-842-2.

Bhaskara Rao, Digumarti (2004). *Issues in School Education.* New Delhi : Discovery Publishing House. ISBN 81-8356-025-3.

Bhaskara Rao, Digumarti, Editor (1996). *Encyclopaedia of Education For All,* 5 volumes. New Delhi : APH Publishing Corporation. ISBN 81-7024-759-4 (set).

*Vol. I* *Education For All : The World Conference.* ISBN 81-7024-760-8

*Vol. II* *Education For All : The EPA-9 Summit.* ISBN 81-7024-761-6

*Vol. II* *Education For All : Quality Education For All.* ISBN 81-7024-762-6.

*Vol. IV* *Education For All : Planning and Monitoring.* ISBN 81-7024-763-4.

*Vol. V* *Education For All : The Indian Scenario.* ISBN 81-7024-764-0.

Bhaskara Rao, Digumarti, Editor (1999). *International Encyclopaedia of AIDS,* 11 Volumes. New Delhi: Discovery Publishing House. ISBN 81-7141-522-6 (set).

*Vol. 1* *Introduction to HIV/AIDS.* ISBN 81-7141-523-7.

*Vol. 2* *HIV/AIDS—Issues and Challenges,* 2 Parts. ISBN 81-7141-524-5.

*Vol. 3* *HIV/AIDS—Socio-economic Realities.* ISBN 81-7141-524-3.

*Vol. 4* *HIV/AIDS—Law Ethics and Human Rights,* 2 Parts. ISBN 81-7141-526-1.

*Vol. 5* *AIDS and NGOs.* ISBN 81-7141-527-X.

*Vol. 6* *AIDS and Home Care.* ISBN 81-7141-528-8.

*Vol. 7* *STD Case Management.* ISBN 81-7141-529-6.

*Vol. 8* *HIV/AIDS Prevention and Care—Teaching Modules for Nurses and Midwives.* ISBN 81-7141-530-X.

*Vol. 9* *HIV Prevention Education for Educational Institutions.* ISBN 81-7141-531-8.

*Vol. 10* *Instructional Modules for AIDS Education.* ISBN 81-7141-532-6.

*Vol. 11* *School Health Education to Prevent AIDS and STD—A Package for Curriculum Planners.* ISBN 81-7141-533-4.

Bhaskara Rao, Digumarti, Editor (2000). *International Encyclopaedia of Human Rights,* 7 Volumes in 13 Parts. New Delhi : Discovery Publishing House. ISBN 81-7141-567-9 (set).

*Vol. 1* *International Instruments of Human Rights,* 2 Parts. ISBN 81-7141-569-4.

*Vol. 2* *Regional Instruments of Human Rights.* ISBN 81-7141-604-7.

*Vol. 3* *Human Rights and the United Nations,* 2 Parts. ISBN 81-7141-605-5.

*Vol. 4* *Fact Files of Human Rights,* 3 Parts. ISBN 81-7141-606-3.

*Vol. 5* *Study Stories of Human Rights,* 3 Parts. ISBN 81-7141-607-3.

*Vol. 6* *International Meetings on Human Rights,* 2 Parts. ISBN 81-714-608-X.

*Vol. 7* *Professional Training in Human Rights.* ISBN 81-7141-609-8.

Bhaskara Rao, Digumarti, editor (2000). *International Encyclopaedia of Science and Technology Education,* 11 Volumes. New Delhi : Discovery Publishing House. ISBN 81-7141-548-2 (set).

*Vol. 1* *Science and Technology Education.* ISBN 81-7141-568-7.

*Vol. 2* *Science Education in Developing Countries.* ISBN 81-7141-569-9.

*Vol. 3* *Organizational Structure of Science.* ISBN 81-7141-570-9.

*Vol. 4* *Science Education in Asia and the Pacific.* ISBN 81-7141-571-7

*Vol. 5* *Science and Technology Education For All.* ISBN 81-7141-572-5.

*Vol. 6* *Values, Ethics, Talent and Girls in Science and Technology Education.* ISBN 81-7141-573-3.

*Vol. 7* *Popularization of Science and Technology Education.* ISBN 81-7141-574-1.

*Vol. 8* *Science, Power and Society.* ISBN 81-7141- 575-X.

*Vol. 9* *Information Technology.* ISBN 81-7141-576-8.

*Vol. 10* *Teacher Training in Science and Technology Education.* ISBN 81-7142-577-6.

*Vol. 11* *Teacher Training in Science and Technology : A Curriculum Framework.* ISBN 81-7141-578-4.

Bhaskara Rao, Digumarti, editor (2000). *Education For All : Achieving the Goal,* 3 Volumes. New Delhi : APH Publishing Corporation. ISBN 81-7648-152-1 (set).

*Vol. I* *The Global Consensus.* ISBN 81-7648-155-6.

*Vol. II* *Mid-decade Review Reports of Regional Seminars.* ISBN 81-7648-154-8.

*Vol. III* *Issues and Trends.* ISBN 81-7648-155-6.

Bhaskara Rao, Digumarti, Editor (2004). *International Encyclopaedia of Learning to Live Together,* 4 Volumes. New Delhi : Discovery Publishing House. ISBN 81-7141-848-1.

*Vol. 1* *International Conference on Learning to Live Together.*

*Vol. 2* *Globalization and Living Together.*

*Vol. 3* *Curriculum for Learning to Live Together.*

*Vol. 4* *Science Education for the Contemporary Society .*

Bhaskara Rao, Digumarti, Editor (2005). *Encyclopaedia of Education For All,* 3 Volumes. New Delhi : Discovery Publishing House. ISBN 81-7141-647-0 (set).

Bhaskara Rao, Digumarti, Editor (2007). *Encyclopaedia of Teacher Education,* 4 Volumes. New Delhi : Discovery Publishing House. ISBN 81-8356-306-6 (set).

Bhaskara Rao, Digumarti, Editor (2007). *Encyclopaedia of Edeucation for Living Together,* 4 Volumes. New Delhi : Discovery Publishing House. ISBN 81-7141-848-1 (set).

Bhaskara Rao, Digumarti, editor (1996). *National Policy on Education,* 2 Volumes. New Delhi: Anmol Publications Pvt. Ltd. ISBN 81-7488-323-1.

Bhaskara Rao, Digumarti, Editor (1996). *Global Perceptions on Peace Education,* 3 Volumes. New Delhi : Discovery Publishing House. ISBN 81-7141-319-6.

Bhaskara Rao, Digumarti, Editor (1997). *Education for the 21st Century.* New Delhi : Discovery Publishing House. ISBN 81-7141-389-7.

Bhaskara Rao, Digumarti, Editor (1997). *Reflections on Scientific Attitude*. New Delhi : Discovery Publishing House. ISBN 81-7141-319-6.

Bhaskara Rao, Digumarti, Editor (1997). *Success Story of a Primary Education Project*. New Delhi : APH Publishing Corporation. ISBN 81-7024-850-7.

Bhaskara Rao, Digumarti, Editor (1997). *World Food Summit*. New Delhi : Discovery Publishing House. ISBN 81-7141-386-2.

Bhaskara Rao, Digumarti, Editor (1997). *Care the Child*, 2 Volumes. New Delhi: Discovery Publishing House. ISBN 81-7141-394-3.

Bhaskara Rao, Digumarti, Editor (1998). *Earth Summit*, 2 Volumes. New Delhi : Discovery Publishing House. ISBN 81-7141-435-4.

Bhaskara Rao, Digumarti, Editor (1998). *Adolescence Education*. New Delhi : Discovery Publishing House. ISBN 81-7141-432-X.

Bhaskara Rao, Digumarti, Editor (1998). *Community and School Nutrition Education*. New Delhi : Discovery Publishing House. ISBN 81-7141-435-4.

Bhaskara Rao, Digumarti, Editor (1998). *District Primary Education Programme*. New Delhi: Discovery Publishing House. ISBN 81-7141-396-X.

Bhaskara Rao, Digumarti, Editor (1998). *National Policy on Education: Towards an Enlightened and Humane Society*. New Delhi : Discovery Publishing House. ISBN 81-7141-426-5.

Bhaskara Rao, Digumarti, Editor (1998). *Reforming School Education*. New Delhi : Discovery Publishing House. ISBN 81-7141-403-6.

Bhaskara Rao, Digumarti, Editor (1998). *Teacher Education in India*. New Delhi : Discovery Publishing House. ISBN 81-7141-406-0.

Bhaskara Rao, Digumarti, Editor (1998). *World Summit for Social Development*. New Delhi : Discovery Publishing House. ISBN 81-7141-420-6.

Bhaskara Rao, Digumarti, Editor (2001). *Nuclear Materials : Issues and Concerns*, 2 volumes. New Delhi : Discovery Publishing House. ISBN 81-7141-611-X.

Bhaskara Rao, Digumarti, Editor (2001). *Distance Education in Different Countries*. New Delhi : APH Publishing Corporation. ISBN 81-7648-229-3.

Bhaskara Rao, Digumarti, Editor (2001). *Decentralised Management of Education : Management of Education in Panchayati Raj and Municipal Bodies.* New Delhi : Discovery Publishing House. ISBN 81-7141-617-9.

Bhaskara Rao, Digumarti, Editor (2001). *Electrochemistry for Environmental Protection.* New Delhi: Discovery Publishing House. ISBN 81-7141-619-5.

Bhaskara Rao, Digumarti, Editor (2001). *Global Educational Studies.* New Delhi : Discovery Publishing House. ISBN 81-7141-616-0.

Bhaskara Rao, Digumarti, Editor (2001). *Global Synthesis of Educational Assessment.* New Delhi : Discovery Publishing House. ISBN 81-7141-613-6.

Bhaskara Rao, Digumarti, Editor (2001). *Jomtein Decade of Education.* New Delhi : Discovery Publishing House. ISBN 81-7141-618-7.

Bhaskara Rao, Digumarti, Editor (2001). *World Conference on Education for All.* New Delhi: APH Publishing Corporation. ISBN 81-7141-274-9.

Bhaskara Rao, Digumarti, Editor (2001). *World Conference on Higher Education.* New Delhi : Discovery Publishing House. ISBN 81-7141-610-1.

Bhaskara Rao, Digumarti, Editor (2001). *World Conference on Science.* New Delhi : Discovery Publishing House. ISBN 81-7141-612-8.

Bhaskara Rao, Digumarti, Editor (2003). *Inspiring Experiences in Teacher Education.* New Delhi : Discovery Publishing House. ISBN 81-7141-656-X.

Bhaskara Rao, Digumarti, Editor (2003). *International Studies in Education,* 3 Volumes. New Delhi : Discovery Publishing House. ISBN 81-7141-647-0.

Bhaskara Rao, Digumarti, Editor (2003). *Military Conversion : Impact on Science and Technology.* New Delhi : Discovery Publishing House. ISBN 81-7141-578-4.

Bhaskara Rao, Digumarti, Editor (2003). *United Nations Millennium Summit.* New Delhi : Discovery Publishing House. ISBN 81-7141-632-2.

Bhaskara Rao, Digumarti, Editor (2003). *World Assembly on Aging.* New Delhi : Discovery Publishing House. ISBN 81-7141-637-3.

Bhaskara Rao, Digumarti, Editor (2003). *World Conference on Human Rights.* New Delhi: Discovery Publishing House. ISBN 81-7141-661-6.

Bhaskara Rao, Digumarti, Editor (2003). *World Education Forum.* New Delhi: Discovery Publishing House. ISBN 81-7141-639-X.

Bhaskara Rao, Digumarti, Editor (2003). *Education, Employment and Human Resource Development.* New Delhi : Discovery Publishing House. ISBN 81-7141- 681-0.

Bhaskara Rao, Digumarti, Editor (2003). *Successful Schooling.* New Delhi : Discovery Publishing House. ISBN 81-7141-677-2.

Bhaskara Rao, Digumarti, Editor (2003). *European Education and Teachers.* New Delhi: Discovery Publishing House. ISBN 81-7141-702-7.

Bhaskara Rao, Digumarti, Editor (2003). *Teachers in a Changing World.* New Delhi : Discovery Publishing House. ISBN 81-7141-694-2.

Bhaskara Rao, Digumarti, Editor (2004). *International Guidelines on Open and Distance Teacher Education.* New Delhi: Discovery Publishing House. ISBN 81-7141-777-9.

Bhaskara Rao, Digumarti, Editor (2004). *Adult Learning in the 21st Century.* New Delhi: Discovery Publishing House. ISBN 81-7141-797-3.

Bhaskara Rao, Digumarti, Editor (2004). *Educational Practices : Research and Recommendations.* New Delhi: Discovery Publishing House. ISBN 81-7141-835-X.

Bhaskara Rao, Digumarti, Editor (2004). *General Secondary Education In the 21st Century.* New Delhi: Discovery Publishing House.

Bhaskara Rao, Digumarti, Editor (2004). *Reforming Secondary Education.* New Delhi: Discovery Publishing House. ISBN 81-7141-843-0.

Bhaskara Rao, Digumarti, Editor (2004). *Human Rights Education.* New Delhi : Discovery Publishing House. ISBN 81-7141-882-1.

Bhaskara Rao, Digumarti, Editor (2004). *United Nations Decade for Human Rights Education.* New Delhi : Discovery Publishing House. ISBN 81-7141-887-2.

Bhaskara Rao, Digumarti, Editor (2004). *Technical and Vocational Education and Training in the 21st Century.* New Delhi : Discovery Publishing House. ISBN 81-7141-984-4.

Bhaskara Rao, Digumarti, Editor (2005). *Encyclopaedia of Education For All*, 3 Volumes. New Delhi : Discovery Publishing House.

Bhaskara Rao, Digumarti, Editor (2011). *Right to Education*. Hyderabad: Neel Kamal Publishers.

Bhaskara Rao, Digumarti, Editor (2011). *International Encyclopaedia of Educational Policies*. Hyderabad : Neel Kamal Publishers.

Bhaskara Rao, Digumarti, Editor (2011). *International Encyclopaedia of Educational Practices*. Hyderabad : Neel Kamal Publishers.

Bhaskara Rao, Digumarti and B.S.V. Dutt, Editors (2003). *Education : Programmes and Policies.* New Delhi : APH Publishing Corporation. ISBN 81-7648-470-9.

Bhaskara Rao, Digumarti, C.A.P. Swamy and B.S.V. Dutt (1997). *Self-evaluation in Student Teaching.* New Delhi : Discovery Publishing House. ISBN 81-7141-374-9.

Bhaskara Rao, Digumarti and C. D. Swarna Lattha, Editors (2006). *Encyclopaedia of Biotechnology*, 5 volumes. New Delhi : Discovery Publishing House. ISBN 81-8356-168-3 (set).

Bhaskara Rao, Digumarti, C. Sridevi and K. Vijaya (1995). *Achievement in Social Studies.* New Delhi: Discovery Publishing House. ISBN 81-7141-281-5.

Bhaskara Rao, Digumarti and D. Naresh Kumar (2004). *School Teacher Effectiveness.* New Delhi : Discovery Publishing House.

Bhaskara Rao, Digumarti and D. Sridhar (2002). *Job Satisfaction of School Teachers.* New Delhi : Discovery Publishing House. ISBN 81-7141-652-7.

Bhaskara Rao, Digumarti and Digumarti Pushpa Latha, Editors (1998). *International Encyclopaedia of Women*, 5 Volumes. New Delhi : Discovery Publishing House. ISBN 81-7141-410-9 (set).

*Vol. 1* *Status of World's Women*. ISBN 81-7141- 494-X.

*Vol. 2* *Women, Education and Empowerment.* ISBN 81-7141-495-1.

*Vol. 3* *Women Challenges and Advancement*. ISBN 81-7141-496-4.

*Vol. 4* *Women and Family Health*. ISBN 81-7141- 497-4.

*Vol. 5* *Women and International Action*. ISBN 81-7141-498-2.

Bhaskara Rao, Digumarti and Digumarti Pushpa Latha (1994). *Achievement in Biology*. New Delhi : Discovery Publishing House. ISBN 81-7141-264-5.

Bhaskara Rao, Digumarti and Digumarti Pushpa Latha (1995). *Achievement in English*. New Delhi : Discovery Publishing House. ISBN 81-7141-283-1.

Bhaskara Rao, Digumarti and Digumarti Pushpa Latha (1994). *Achievement in Science*. New Delhi : Discovery Publishing House. ISBN 81-7141-280-70.

Bhaskara Rao, Digumarti and Digumarti Pushpa Latha (1995). *Achievement in Mathematics*. New Delhi : Discovery Publishing House. ISBN 81-7141-278-5.

Bhaskara Rao, Digumarti and Digumarti Pushpa Latha (2004). *Education for Women*. New Delhi : Discovery Publishing House. ISBN 81-7141-873-2.

Bhaskara Rao, Digumarti, Digumarti Pushpa Latha and Digumarthi Harshitha, Editors (2001). *Biological Warfare*. New Delhi: Discovery Publishing House. ISBN 81-7141-597-0.

Bhaskara Rao, Digumarti, Digumarti Pushpa Latha and Digumarthi Harshitha, Editors (2001). *Women as Educators*. New Delhi: Discovery Publishing House. ISBN 81-7141-602-0.

Bhaskara Rao, Digumarti and Digumarthi Harshitha (2004). *Adjustment of Adolescents*. New Delhi: APH Publishing House. ISBN 81-7648-836-8.

Bhaskara Rao, Digumarti and Digumarthi Harshitha, Editors (2001). *Education in India*. New Delhi: APH Publishing House. ISBN 81-7648-207-2.

Bhaskara Rao, Digumarti, Digumarti Pushpa Latha and Digumarthi Harshitha, Editors (2001). *Assessing Learning Achievement*. New Delhi : Discovery Publishing House. ISBN 81-7141-601-2.

Bhaskara Rao, Digumarti, Digumarti Pushpa Latha and Digumarthi Harshitha, Editors (2001). *Energy Security*. New Delhi : Discovery Publishing House. ISBN 81-7141-598-9.

Bhaskara Rao, Digumarti, Digumarthi Harshitha and K.R.S. Sambasiva Rao, Editors (1999). *Advanced Biotechnology*. New Delhi : Discovery Publishing House. ISBN 81-7141-516-4.

Bhaskara Rao, Digumarti and K.R.S. Sambasiva Rao, Editors (1996). *Current Trends in Indian Education.* New Delhi : Discovery Publishing House. ISBN 81-7141-311-0.

Bhaskara Rao, Digumarti and D. Naresh Kumar (2004). *School Teacher Effectiveness.* New Delhi : Discovery Publishing House. ISBN 81-7141-782-5.

Bhaskara Rao, Digumarti and E. Sreekanth Babu (2004). *Educational Interests of School Students.* New Delhi : Discovery Publishing House. ISBN 81-7141-837-6.

Bhaskara Rao, Digumarti and K. Vijaya (1995). *A Text Book Evaluation.* Ambala Cantt : The Associated Publishers.

Bhaskara Rao, Digumarti and M.A. Fayaz (2004). *Problems of Primary School Drop-outs.* New Delhi : Discovery Publishing House. ISBN 81-7141- 834-1.

Bhaskara Rao, Digumarti and N.V.M. Mohana Rao (2002). *Problems of Mentally Handicapped Children.* New Delhi : Discovery Publishing House. ISBN 81-7141- 645-4.

Bhaskara Rao, Digumarti and S. Chandra Mohan (2002). *Sports Management.* New Delhi : APH Publishing House. ISBN 81-7648-467-9.

Bhaskara Rao, Digumarti and S.A. Khader (2004). *Problems of Private School Teachers.* New Delhi : Discovery Publishing Home. ISBN 81-7141-838-4.

Bhaskara Rao, Digumarti and S.A. Khader (2004). *School Education in India.* New Delhi : Discovery Publishing Home. ISBN 81-7141-849-X.

Bhaskara Rao, Digumarti and Sk. Johni Basha (2004). *Teachers' Population Education Awareness.* New Delhi : Discovery Publishing House. ISBN 81-7141-832-5.

Bhaskara Rao, Digumarti, V.V. Rao, V.V. Lakshmi and V.V. Krishna, Editors (1999). *Status and Advancement of Women.* New Delhi: APH Publishing Corporation. ISBN 81-7648-169-6.

Babu, P.C., Author and Digumarti Bhaskara Rao, Editor (2004). *Flowers of Wisdom.* New Delhi : Discovery Publishing House. ISBN 81-7141-695-0.

Babu, P.C., Author and Digumarti Bhaskara Rao, Editor (2008). *Worlds of Wisdom.* New Delhi: Discovery Publishing House.

Bujji Babu, K., Author and Digumarti Bhaskara Rao, Editor (2007). *Teaching Aptitude of Primary School Teachers.* New Delhi: Sonali Publications. ISBN 81-8411-083-9.

Amala, P. A. and Anupama, P., Authors and Digumarti Bhaskara Rao, Editor (2004). *History of Education.* New Delhi : Discovery Publishing House. ISBN 81-7141-860-0.

Bhagya Lakshmi, L., Author and Digumarti Bhaskara Rao, Editor (2000). *Reading and Comprehension.* New Delhi : Discovery Publishing House. ISBN 81-7141-543-1.

Bhasha, S.A., Author and Digumarti Bhaskara Rao, Editor (2004). *Methods of Teaching Geography.* New Delhi : Discovery Publishing House. ISBN 81-7141-807-4.

Bhuvaneswara Lakshmi, Gadde, Author and Digumarti Bhaskara Rao, Editor (2000). *Attitude Towards Science.* New Delhi : Discovery Publishing House. ISBN 81-7141-541-6.

Bhuvaneswara Lakshmi, G., Author and Digumarti Bhaskara Rao, Editor (2004). *Methods of Teaching Life Science.* New Delhi : Discovery Publishing House. ISBN 81-7141-804-X.

Bhuvaneswara Lakshmi, G. and K. Subba Rao, Authors and Digumarti Bhaskara Rao, Editor (2004). *Methods of Teaching Biology.* New Delhi : Discovery Publishing House. ISBN 81-7141-914-3.

Chary, K.V.N.B., Author and Digumarti Bhaskara Rao, Editor (2006). *Techniques of Teaching Physics.* New Delhi : Sonali Publications. ISBN 81-8411-046-4.

Chowdary, S.B.J.R. and Naga Raju, Authors and Digumarti Bhaskara Rao, Editor (2004). *Mastery of Teaching Skills.* New Delhi : Discovery Publishing House.

Dayakara Reddy, V. and Digumarti Bhaskara Rao, Editors (2006). *Value-oriented Education.* New Delhi : Discovery Publishing House.

Devraj, T.A.S., Author and Digumarti Bhaskara Rao, Editor (1997). *Trace Analysis of Uranium and Thorium.* New Delhi : Discovery Publishing House. ISBN 81-7141-375-7.

Durga Rani, K., Author and Digumarti Bhaskara Rao, Editor (2000). *Educational Aspirations and Scientific Attitudes.* New Delhi : Discovery Publishing House. ISBN 81-7141-555-5.

Dutt, B.S.V. and Digumarti Bhaskara Rao (2001). *Empowering Primary Teachers.* New Delhi : Discovery Publishing House. ISBN 81-7141-615-2.

Dutt, B.S.V., Author and Digumarti Bhaskara Rao, Editor (2004). *Comparative Education.* New Delhi: Discovery Publishing House. ISBN 81-7141-912-7.

Ediger, Marlow and Digumarti Bhaskara Rao, Editors (2006). *Encyclopaedia of School Education,* 5 Volumes. New Delhi : Discovery Publishing House. ISBN 81-8356-308-2 (set).

Ediger, Marlow and Digumarti Bhaskara Rao, Editors (2006). *Encyclopaedia of School Administration,* 4 Volumes. New Delhi : Discovery Publishing House. ISBN 81-8356-307-4 (set).

Ediger, Marlow and Digumarti Bhaskara Rao, Editors (2007). *Encyclopaedia of School Curriculum,* 10 Volumes. New Delhi : Discovery Publishing House. ISBN 81-8356-305-8 (set).

Ediger, Marlow and Digumarti Bhaskara Rao, Editors (2007). *Encyclopaedia of Teaching,* 8 Volumes. New Delhi : Discovery Publishing House. ISBN 81-8356-305-8 (set).

Marlow Ediger and Digumarti Bhaskara Rao, Editors (2006). *Encyclopaedia of School Education,* 5 Volumes. New Delhi : Discovery Publishing House. ISBN 81-8356-308-2 (set).

Marlow Ediger and Digumarti Bhaskara Rao, Editors (2006). *Encyclopaedia of School Administration,* 4 Volumes. New Delhi : Discovery Publishing House. ISBN 81-8356-307-4 (set).

Ediger, Marlow and Digumarti Bhaskara Rao (1996). *Science Curriculum.* New Delhi: Discovery Publishing House. ISBN 81-7141-321-8.

Ediger, Marlow and Digumarti Bhaskara Rao (2000). *Teaching Mathematics Successfully.* New Delhi : Discovery Publishing House. ISBN 81-7141-552-0.

Ediger, Marlow and Digumarti Bhaskara Rao (2001). *Teaching Science Successfully.* New Delhi : Discovery Publishing House. ISBN 81-7141-600-4.

Ediger, Marlow and Digumarti Bhaskara Rao (2001). *Teaching Social Studies Successfully.* New Delhi : Discovery Publishing House. ISBN 81-7141-596-2.

Ediger, Marlow and Digumarti Bhaskara Rao (2002). *Philosophy and Curriculum.* New Delhi: Discovery Publishing House. ISBN 81-7141-631-4.

Ediger, Marlow and Digumarti Bhaskara Rao (2002). *Improving School Administration.* New Delhi : Discovery Publishing House. ISBN 81-7141-633-0

Ediger, Marlow and Digumarti Bhaskara Rao (2002). *Elementary Curriculum.* New Delhi : Discovery Publishing House. ISBN 81-7141-658-6.

Ediger, Marlow and Digumarti Bhaskara Rao (2003). *Language Arts Curriculum.* New Delhi : Discovery Publishing House. ISBN 81-7141-657-8.

Ediger, Marlow and Digumarti Bhaskara Rao (2003). *Psychology and Curriculum.* New Delhi : Discovery Publishing House. ISBN 81-7141-691-8.

Ediger, Marlow and Digumarti Bhaskara Rao (2003). *Teaching Language Arts Successfully.* New Delhi : Discovery Publishing House.

Ediger, Marlow and Digumarti Bhaskara Rao (2003). *School Curriculum and Administration.* New Delhi : Discovery Publishing House. ISBN 81-7141-709-4.

Ediger, Marlow and Digumarti Bhaskara Rao (2003). *Teaching Mathematics in Elementary Schools.* New Delhi : Discovery Publishing House. ISBN 81-7141-687-X.

Ediger, Marlow and Digumarti Bhaskara Rao (2003). *Teaching Science in Elementary Schools.* New Delhi: Discovery Publishing House. ISBN 81-7141-698-5.

Ediger, Marlow and Digumarti Bhaskara Rao (2003). *School Curriculum and Administration.* New Delhi : Discovery Publishing House. ISBN 81-7141-709-4.

Ediger, Marlow and Digumarti Bhaskara Rao (2003). *Elementary Curriculum Improvement.* New Delhi : Discovery Publishing House. ISBN 81-7141-740-X.

Ediger, Marlow and Digumarti Bhaskara Rao (2004). *School Organisation.* New Delhi : Discovery Publishing House. ISBN 81-7141-843-0.

Ediger, Marlow and Digumarti Bhaskara Rao (2004). *Relevancy in Elementary Curriculum.* New Delhi : Discovery Publishing House. ISBN 81-7141-845-9.

Ediger, Marlow and Digumarti Bhaskara Rao (2005). *Quality School Education.* New Delhi : Discovery Publishing House. ISBN 81-8356-022-9.

Ediger, Marlow and Digumarti Bhaskara Rao (2006). *Successful School Education.* New Delhi : Discovery Publishing House. ISBN 81-8356-054-7.

Ediger, Marlow and Digumarti Bhaskara Rao (2006). *Successful School Administration.* New Delhi : Discovery Publishing House. ISBN 81-8356-046-6.

Ediger, Marlow and Digumarti Bhaskara Rao (2006). *Issues in School Curruculum.* New Delhi : Discovery Publishing House. ISBN 81-8356-052-0.

Ediger, Marlow and Digumarti Bhaskara Rao (2006). *Community College—Curriculum and Teaching.* New Delhi : Discovery Publishing House. ISBN 81-8356-053-9.

Ediger, Marlow and Digumarti Bhaskara Rao (2006). *Administration of Schools.* New Delhi : Discovery Publishing House.

Ediger, Marlow and Digumarti Bhaskara Rao (2006). *Reading Curriculum and Instruction.* New Delhi : Discovery Publishing House.

Ediger, Marlow and Digumarti Bhaskara Rao (2006). *Curriculum Organisation.* New Delhi: Discovery Publishing House.

Ediger, Marlow and Digumarti Bhaskara Rao (2006). *Curriculum of School Subjects.* New Delhi : Discovery Publishing House.

Ediger, Marlow, B.S.V. Dutt and Digumarti Bhaskara Rao (2003). *Teaching English Successfully.* New Delhi : Discovery Publishing House. ISBN 81-7141-707-8.

Ediger, Marlow and Digumarti Bhaskara Rao (2007). *School Science Education.* New Delhi : Discovery Publishing House. ISBN 81-8356-352-X.

Ediger, Marlow and Digumarti Bhaskara Rao (2007). *Language Arts Education*. New Delhi : Discovery Publishing House. ISBN 81-8356-333-3.

Ediger, Marlow and Digumarti Bhaskara Rao (2010). *Effective Schooling*. New Delhi : Discovery Publishing House. ISBN 978-81-8356-613-1.

Ediger, Marlow and Digumarti Bhaskara Rao (2010). *Effective School Curriculum*. New Delhi : Discovery Publishing House. ISBN 978-81-8356-585-1.

Ediger, Marlow and Digumarti Bhaskara Rao (2010). *Essays on Teaching Science*. New Delhi : Discovery Publishing House.

Ediger, Marlow and Digumarti Bhaskara Rao (2010). *Essays on Teaching Social Studies*. New Delhi : Discovery Publishing House.

Ediger, Marlow and Digumarti Bhaskara Rao (2010). *Essays on Teaching Reading*. New Delhi : Discovery Publishing House.

Ediger, Marlow and Digumarti Bhaskara Rao (2010). *Essays on Teaching Mathematics*. New Delhi : Discovery Publishing House.

Ediger, Marlow and Digumarti Bhaskara Rao (2010). *Essays on Teaching*. New Delhi : Discovery Publishing House.

Elizabeth, M.E.S., Author and Digumarti Bhaskara Rao, Editor (2004). *Methods of Teaching English*. New Delhi : Discovery Publishing House. ISBN 81-7141-809-0.

Elizabeth, M.E.S., Author and Digumarti Bhaskara Rao, Editor (2004). *Acquisition of English Vocabulary*. New Delhi : Discovery Publishing House. ISBN 81-7141- .

Fatima, Sk. Author and Digumarti Bhaskara Rao, Editor (2007). *Reasoning Ability of School Students*. New Delhi : Discovery Publishing House.

Fatima, Sk. and Digumarti Bhaskara Rao (2008). *Reasoning Ability of Adolescent Students*. New Delhi : Sonali Publications.

Gopala Krishna, M., author and Digumarti Bhaskara Rao, editor (2007). *Techniques of Teaching Physical Education*. New Delhi : Sonali Publications. ISBN 81-8411-044-8.

Gopala Krishna, M., author and Digumarti Bhaskara Rao, editor (2007). *Techniques of Teaching Education*. New Delhi : Sonali Publications. ISBN 81-8411-062-6.

Harshitha, Digumarthi, Author and Digumarti Bhaskara Rao, Editor (2004). *Methods of Teaching Information Technology.* New Delhi : Discovery Publishing House. ISBN 81-7141-805-8.

Harshitha, Digumarthi, Author and Digumarti Bhaskara Rao, Editor (2007).. *Techniques of Teaching Computer Science.* New Delhi : Sonali Publications. ISBN 81-8411-036-7.

Indira Devi, Author and J. Prasanth Kumar and Digumarti Bhaskara Rao, Editors (2004). *Values in Language Text Books.* New Delhi : APH Publishing Corporation.

Jalaja Kumari, C., Author and Digumarti Bhaskara Rao, Editor (2004). *Methods of Teaching Educational Technology.* New Delhi : Discovery Publishing House. ISBN 81-7141-810-4.

Jalaja Kumari, C., Author and Digumarti Bhaskara Rao, Editor (2007). *Job Satisfaction of Teachers.* New Delhi : Discovery Publishing House.

Janardhan Reddy, B., Author and Digumarti Bhaskara Rao, Editor (2006). *Techniques of Teaching Sociology.* New Delhi : Sonali Publications. ISBN 81-8411-042-1.

Jayasree, K., Author and Digumarti Bhaskara Rao, Editor (1999). *Correlates of Socialisation.* New Delhi : Discovery Publishing House. ISBN 81-7141-517-2.

Jayasree, K., Author and Digumarti Bhaskara Rao, Editor (2004). *Methods of Teaching Science.* New Delhi : Discovery Publishing House. ISBN 81-7141-801-5.

John Babu, C., Author and T.J.R. Prasad, G.M. Madhukar and Digumarti Bhaskara Rao, Editors (2004). *Problem Solving in Mathematics.* New Delhi : APH Publishing Corporation. ISBN 81-7648-273-0.

Joseph Raju, B and G.A. Anitha, Authors and Digumarti Bhaskara Rao, Editor (2004). *Population Education.* New Delhi : Sonali Publications. ISBN 81-88836-31-3.

Jyosthana, M., Author and Digumarti Bhaskara Rao, Editor (2011). *Achievement Motivation and Achievement in English of School Students.* New Delhi : Discovery Publishing House.

Lalitha, T., Author and K.S. Prabhakaram, D.S.N. Sastry and Digumarti Bhaskara Rao, Editors (2004). *Educational Philosophic Beliefs.* New Delhi: Discovery Publishing House. ISBN 81-7141-765-5.

Krishna, G., Author and Digumarti Bhaskara Rao, Editor (2006). *Techniques of Teaching Physical Education.* New Delhi : Discovery Publishing House. ISBN 81-8411-044-8.

Kumar Raja, G., Author and Digumarti Bhaskara Rao, Editor (2007). *Principles of Primary School.* New Delhi : Sonali Publications. ISBN 81-8411-054-5.

Lakshmi Kumari, V., Author and Digumarti Bhaskara Rao, Editor (2006). *Techniques of Teaching Home Science.* New Delhi : Sonali Publications. ISBN 81-8411-048-0.

Madhava, K., Author and Digumarti Bhaskara Rao, Editor (2008). *Personality of Adolescent Students.* New Delhi: Sonali Publications.

Madhu Bala, Jampala, Author and Digumarti Bhaskara Rao, Editor (2004). *Methods of Teaching Exceptional Children.* New Delhi: Discovery Publishing House. ISBN 81-7141-802-3.

Mallikarjuna Reddy, V., Author and Digumarti Bhaskara Rao, Editor (2011). *Teaching Aptitude, Social Adjustment and Job Satisfaction of Science Teachers.* New Delhi: Discovery Publishing House.

Marja, Talvi and Digumarti Bhaskara Rao, Editors (1996). *Educational Leadership and Social Changes.* New Delhi : Discovery Publishing House. ISBN 81-7141-320-X.

Naga Kumari, U., Author and Digumarti Bhaskara Rao, Editor (2008). *Science Process Skills of School Students.* New Delhi : Sonali Publications.

Nageswara Rao, S. and M. Srihari, Authors and Digumarti Bhaskara Rao, Editor (2004). *Guidance and Counselling.* New Delhi : Discovery Publishing House. ISBN 81-7141-840-6.

Nageswara Rao, S., Author and Digumarti Bhaskara Rao, Editor (2006). *Techniques of Teaching Psychology.* New Delhi : Sonali Publications. ISBN 81-8411-040-5.

Nageswara Rao, S. and P. Sridhar, Authors and Digumarti Bhaskara Rao, Editor (2004). *Methods and Techniques of Teaching.* New Delhi: Sonali Publications. ISBN 81-88836-33-8.

Nirmala Jyothi, M., Author and Digumarti Bhaskara Rao, Editor (2003). *Non-detention System in School Education.* New Delhi : Discovery Publishing House. ISBN 81-7141-654-3.

Padma Tulasi, G., Author and Digumarti Bhaskara Rao, Editor (2004). *Methods of Teaching Elementary Science.* New Delhi : Discovery Publishing House. ISBN 81-7141-871-6.

Pala Prasada Rao, V., Author and K. N. Rani and D. Bhaskara Rao, Editors (2004).*India Pakistan : Partition Perspectives in Indo-English Novels.* New Delhi: Discovery Publishing House. ISBN 81-7141-871-6.

Pala Prasada Rao, V., Author and D. Bhaskara Rao, Editors (2008). *Functioning of Autonomous Colleges.* New Delhi : Sonali Publications.

Pitchi Reddy, M., Author and Digumarti Bhaskara Rao, Editor (2007). *Techniques of Teaching Social Sciences.* New Delhi : Sonali Publications. ISBN 81-8411-066-X.

Prasad Babu, B., Author and P. Madhu and Digumarti Bhaskara Rao, Editors (2006). *Psychological Adjustment and Well-being.* New Delhi: Discovery Publishing House. ISBN 81-8356-204-3.

Prasad Babu, B., Author and M.V.R. Raju and Digumarti Bhaskara Rao, Editors (2006). *Behavioural Problems of School Children.* New Delhi: Discovery Publishing House. ISBN 81-8356-206-X.

Prabhakaram, K.S., Author and Digumarti Bhaskara Rao, Editors (1998). *Concept Attainment Model in Mathematics Teaching.* New Delhi : Discovery Publishing House. ISBN 81-7141-424-9.

Prasanth Kumar, J., Author and Digumarti Bhaskara Rao, Editor (1998). *Effectiveness of Distance Education System.* New Delhi : Discovery Publishing House. ISBN 81-7141-437-0.

Prasanth Kumar, J., Author and Digumarti Bhaskara Rao, Editor (2004). *Methods of Teaching Civics.* New Delhi : Discovery Publishing House. ISBN 81-7141-806-6.

Prasanth Kumar, J., Author and G. Sundara Rao and Digumarti Bhaskara Rao, Editors (2000). *Open University Student Support Services.* New Delhi : Discovery Publishing House. ISBN 81-7141-550-4.

Raja Kumari, M.A. and D.R.S. Sundari, Authors and Digumarti Bhaskara Rao, Editor (2004). *Special Education.* New Delhi : Discovery Publishing House. ISBN 81-7141-846-5.

Raja Kumari, M.A. and D.R.S. Sundari, Authors and Digumarti Bhaskara Rao, Editor (2004). *Methods of Teaching Educational Psychology.* New Delhi : Discovery Publishing House.

Ramatulasamma, K., Author and Digumarti Bhaskara Rao, Editor (2002). *Job Satisfaction of Teacher Educators.* New Delhi : Discovery Publishing House. ISBN 81-7141-655-1.

Rama Krishnaiah, D., Author and Digumarti Bhaskara Rao, Editor (1998). *Job Satisfaction of College Teachers.* New Delhi : Discovery Publishing House. ISBN 81-7141-438-9.

Rama Kumar Ratnam, M.V., Author and Digumarti Bhaskara Rao, Editor (1998). *Dukkha : Suffering in Early Buddhism.* New Delhi: Discovery Publishing House. ISBN 81-7141-653-5.

Rama Krishna Prasad and P. Vide Sagar, Authors and Digumarti Bhaskara Rao, Editor (2004). *Methods of Teaching Physical Education.* New Delhi : Discovery Publishing House.

Rama Seshaiah, P. Author and Digumarti Bhaskara Rao, Editor (2004). *Methods of Teaching Home Science.* New Delhi : Discovery Publishing House. ISBN 81-7141-916-X.

Rama Swamy, K., Author and Digumarti Bhaskara Rao, Editor (2007). *Techniques of Teaching Environmental Science.* New Delhi : Sonali Publications. ISBN 81-8411-035-9.

Ramesh, A.R., Author and Digumarti Bhaskara Rao, Editor (2006). *Techniques of Teaching Commerce.* New Delhi : Sonali Publications. ISBN 81-8411-043-X.

Ramesh, Ghanta and Digumarti Bhaskara Rao, Editors (1998). *Environmental Education : Problems and Prospects.* New Delhi: Discovery Publishing House. ISBN 81-7141-423-0.

Ranga Rao, B., Author and Digumarti Bhaskara Rao, Editor (2007). *Techniques of Teaching Economics.* New Delhi : Sonali Publications. ISBN 81-8411-056-1.

Ranga Rao, R., Author and Digumarti Bhaskara Rao, Editor (2004). *Methods of Teacher Teaching.* New Delhi : Discovery Publishing House. ISBN 81-7141-812-0.

Rani, S.S., Author and Digumarti Bhaskara Rao, Editor (2006). *Techniques of Teaching Botany.* New Delhi : Sonali Publications. ISBN 81-8411-037-5.

Rathaiah, Lavu and Digumarti Bhaskara Rao, Editors (1996), *International Innovations in Education.* New Delhi : Discovery Publishing House. ISBN 81-7141-359-5.

Rathaiah, Lavu and Digumarti Bhaskara Rao (1997). *Achievement Correlates.* New Delhi: Discovery Publishing House. ISBN 81-7141-385-4.

Ravi Krishna, M., Author and Digumarti Bhaskara Rao, Editor (2004). *Examination System.* New Delhi : Discovery Publishing House. ISBN 81-7141-824-4.

Ravi Kumar, M., Author and Digumarti Bhaskara Rao, Editor (2004). *Methods of Teaching Computer Science.* New Delhi : Discovery Publishing House. ISBN 81-7141-823-6.

Rudramamba, B., Author and Digumarti Bhaskara Rao, Editor (2003). *Problems of Teaching.* New Delhi : APH Publishing Corporation. ISBN 81-7648-462-8.

Rudramamba, B. and V. Lakshmi Kumari, Authors and Digumarti Bhaskara Rao, Editor (2004). *Methods of Teaching Economics.* New Delhi : Discovery Publishing House. ISBN 81-7141-900-3.

Sambasiva Rao, P., Author and Digumarti Bhaskara Rao, Editor (2007). *Techniques of Teaching Psychology.* New Delhi : Sonali Publications. ISBN 81-8411-040-5.

Sanjeeva Rao, P.C., Author and Digumarti Bhaskara Rao, Editor (1996). *A Text Book of Geology.* New Delhi : Discovery Publishing House. ISBN 81-7141-313-7.

Santhanam, T., B. Prasad Babu and S. Sugandhi, Authors and Digumarti Bhaskara Rao, Editor (2007). *Children with Learning Disabilities.* New Delhi : Sonali Publications. ISBN 81-8411-077-4.

Santhanam, T., B. Prasad Babu and S. Sugandhi, Authors and Digumarti Bhaskara Rao, Editor (2008). *Learning Disabilities and Remedial Programmes.* New Delhi : Discovery Publishing House.

Sarala, M.M.O., Author and Digumarti Bhaskara Rao, Editor (2006). *Techniques of Teaching English.* New Delhi : Sonali Publications. ISBN 81-8411-047-2.

Satya Narayana, G., Author and Digumarti Bhaskara Rao, Editor (2008). *Attitude towards Social Studies and Achievement in Social Studies.* New Delhi : Sonali Publications.

Satya Narayana, V., Author and Digumarti Bhaskara Rao, Editor (2001). *Physical Education, Social Attitudes and Leadership Qualities.* New Delhi : Discovery Publishing House. ISBN 81-7141-593-8.

Satya Narayana, P.V.V. and G. Krishna, Authors and Digumarti Bhaskara Rao, Editor (2004). *Curriculum Development and Management.* New Delhi : Discovery Publishing House. ISBN 81-7141-813-9.

Shamsuddin, Sk. and V. Dayakara Reddy, Authors and Digumarti Bhaskara Rao, Editor (2007). *Academic Achievement and Values.* New Delhi : Discovery Publishing House.

Singh, Y.C., Author and Digumarti Bhaskara Rao, Editor (2006). *Techniques of Teaching Science.* New Delhi : Sonali Publications. ISBN 81-8411-041-3.

Sirisha Rani, S., Author and Digumarti Bhaskara Rao, Editor (2007). *Techniques of Teaching Botany.* New Delhi : Sonali Publications. ISBN 81-8411-037-5.

Sivaratnam Reddy, M., Author and Digumarti Bhaskara Rao, Editor (2004). *Creativity in College Students.* New Delhi : Discovery Publishing House. ISBN 81-7141-697-7.

Siva Lakshmi, G.V. and G.L. Subbaiah, Authors and Digumarti Bhaskara Rao, Editor (2004). *Methods of Teaching Environmental Science.* New Delhi: Discovery Publishing House. ISBN 81-7141-839-2.

Srinivas, G. and Digumarti Bhaskara Rao (2007). *Anxiety of Prospective Teachers.* New Delhi : Sonali Publications. ISBN 81-8411-084-7.

Srinivas, G. and Digumarti Bhaskara Rao (2011). *Intelligence and Personality of Prospective Teachers.* New Delhi : Discovery Publishing House.

Srinivas, M. and I. Prasada Rao, Authors and Digumarti Bhaskara Rao, Editor (2004). *Methods of Teaching History.* New Delhi : Discovery Publishing House.

Srinivas Rao, P., Author and Digumarti Bhaskara Rao, Editor (2007). *Principles of Secondary School.* New Delhi : Sonali Publications. ISBN 81-8411-058-8.

Srinivasulu, K., Author and Digumarti Bhaskara Rao, Editor (2011). *Achievement Motivation and Academic Achievement of Alcoholic and Non-alcoholic College Students.* New Delhi : Discovery Publishing House.

Srinivasulu Reddy, M. and K.R.S. Sambasiva Rao, Authors and Digumarti Bhaskara Rao, Editor (1999). *A Text Book of Aquaculture*. New Delhi : Discovery Publishing House. ISBN 81-7141-482-6.

Srinivasa Rao, Mandalapu, Author and Digumarti Bhaskara Rao, Editor (2003). *Achievement Motivation and Achievement in Mathematics*. New Delhi : Discovery Publishing House. ISBN 81-7141-674-8.

Srihari, M., Author and Digumarti Bhaskara Rao, Editor (2003). *Values of Prospective Teachers*. New Delhi : Discovery Publishing House. ISBN 81-8356-328-7.

Subba Rao, K., Author and Digumarti Bhaskara Rao, Editor (2007). *School Education Policy*. New Delhi : Discovery Publishing House. ISBN 81-8356-285-X.

Subba Rao, K., Author and Digumarti Bhaskara Rao, Editor (2007). *Education Planning*. New Delhi : Sonali Publications. ISBN 81-8411-053-7.

Subramanyam, N.R., Author and Digumarti Bhaskara Rao, Editor (2011). *Effectiveness of In-service Training Programmes*. New Delhi : Discovery Publishing House.

Sudhakar Reddy, Y., Author and Digumarti Bhaskara Rao, Editor (2003). *Creativity in Adolescents*. New Delhi : Discovery Publishing House. ISBN 81-7141-659-4.

Sunil Kumar, K. and K. Rama Krishana, Authors and Digumarti Bhaskara Rao, Editor (2004). *Methods of Teaching Chemistry*. New Delhi : Discovery Publishing House. ISBN 81-7141-913-5.

Suneetha, G., Author and Digumarti Bhaskara Rao, Editor (2004). *Environmental Awareness of School Students*. New Delhi : Sonali Publications. ISBN 81-8411-085-5.

Sunita, E. and R. Sambasiva Rao, Authors and Digumarti Bhaskara Rao, Editor (2004). *Methods of Teaching Mathematics*. New Delhi : Discovery Publishing House. ISBN 81-7141-915-1.

Surya Madhava, I., Author and Digumarti Bhaskara Rao, Editor (2006). *Techniques of Teaching Geography*. New Delhi : Sonali Publications. . ISBN 81-8411-034-0.

Surya Madhava, I., Author and Digumarti Bhaskara Rao, Editor (2007). *Techniques of Teaching Political Science.* New Delhi : Sonali Publications. ISBN 81-8411-061-8.

Swamy, K.R., Author and Digumarti Bhaskara Rao, Editor (2006). *Techniques of Teaching Environmental Science.* New Delhi : Sonali Publications. ISBN 81-8411-035-9.

Swarna Jyothi, K., Author and Digumarti Bhaskara Rao, Editor (2007). *Educational Research.* New Delhi : Sonali Publications. ISBN 81-8411-063-4.

Swarna Latha, C.D., and Digumarti Bhaskara Rao, Editors (2006). *Encyclopaedia of Biotechnology,* 5 volumes. New Delhi : Discovery Publishing House. ISBN 81-8356-168-3.

Swarupa Rani, T. and J.R. Priyadarshini, Authors and Digumarti Bhaskara Rao, Editor (2004). *Educational Measurement and Evaluation.* New Delhi : Discovery Publishing House. ISBN 81-7141-859-7.

Vanaja, M., Author and Digumarti Bhaskara Rao, Editor (1999). *Inquiry Training Model.* New Delhi : Discovery Publishing House. ISBN 81-7141-515-6.

Vanaja, M., Author and Digumarti Bhaskara Rao, Editor (2004). *Methods of Teaching Physics.* New Delhi : Discovery Publishing House. ISBN 81-7141-867-8

Vanaja, M. and N. Sneha Latha, Authors and Digumarti Bhaskara Rao, Editor (2004). *Student Shyness.* New Delhi : APH Publishing Corporation.

Valeri V. Koustiouk, Author and Digumarti Bhaskara Rao, Editor (2002). *A Text Book of Cryogenics.* New Delhi : Discovery Publishing House. ISBN 81-7141-642-X.

Vamsi Krishna, V., Author and Digumarti Bhaskara Rao, Editor (2004). *School Psychology.* New Delhi: Discovery Publishing House. ISBN 81-7141-880-5.

Veena Kumari, Balusu and Digumarti Bhaskara Rao (1996). *Operation Black Board.* New Delhi : APH Publishing Corporation. ISBN 81-7024-711-X.

Veena Kumari, Balusu, Author and Digumarti Bhaskara Rao, Editor (2004). *Methods of Teaching Social Studies.* New Delhi : Discovery Publishing House. ISBN 81-7141-899-6.

Veena Kumari, Balusu, Author and Digumarti Bhaskara Rao, Editor (2000). *Psycho-Social Correlates of Achievement.* New Delhi : Discovery Publishing House. ISBN 81-7141-547-4.

Venkata Rao, B., Author and Digumarti Bhaskara Rao, Editor (2007). *Techniques of Teaching Chemistry.* New Delhi : Sonali Publications. ISBN 81-8411-057-X.

Venkata Rao, P. and Digumarti Bhaskara Rao (1989). *A Text Book of Zoology—Junior Intermediate.* Guntur : Vignan Publishers.

Venkata Rao, P. and Digumarti Bhaskara Rao (1989). *A Text Book of Zoology—Senior Intermediate.* Guntur : Vignan Publishers.

Venkateswara Rao, V., Author and Digumarti Bhaskara Rao, Editor (2004). *Problems of Education.* New Delhi : Discovery Publishing House. ISBN 81-7141-841-4.

Venkateswara Rao, V., V. Vijaya Lakshmi and V. Vamsi Krishna, Authors and Digumarti Bhaskara Rao, Editor (2004). *Education For All.* New Delhi : Sonali Publications. ISBN 81-88836-30-3.

Venkateswara Rao, V., V. Vijaya Lakshmi and V. Vamsi Krishna, Authors and Digumarti Bhaskara Rao, Editor (2004). *Education in India.* New Delhi : Sonali Publications. ISBN 81-88836-858-9.

Venkateswara Reddy, L. and Narayana, M. L., Authors and Digumarti Bhaskara Rao, Editor (2004). *Education for Dalits.* New Delhi : Discovery Publishing House. ISBN 81-7141-872-4.

Venkateswara Reddy, L. and Narayana, M. L, Authors and Digumarti Bhaskara Rao, Editor (2004). *Methods of Teaching Rural Sociology.* New Delhi : Discovery Publishing House. ISBN 81-7141-811-2.

Venkateswarlu, K. and S.J. Basha, Authors and Digumarti Bhaskara Rao, Editor (2004). *Methods of Teaching Commerce.* New Delhi : Discovery Publishing House. ISBN 81-7141-808-2.

Venugopala Rao, K., Author and Digumarti Bhaskara Rao, Editor (2000). *Teacher Morale in Secondary Schools.* New Delhi : Discovery Publishing House. ISBN 81-7141-551-2.

Venugopala Rao, K., Author and Digumarti Bhaskara Rao, Editor (2007). *Techniques of Teaching History.* New Delhi : Sonali Publications. ISBN 81-8411-059-6.

Vidya, C., Author and Digumarti Bhaskara Rao, Editor (1996). *A Text Book of Nutrition.* New Delhi : Discovery Publishing House. ISBN 81-7141-309-9.

Vimala, T.D., B. Prasad Babu and Digumarti Bhaskara Rao, Editors (2007). *Stress, Coping and Management.* New Delhi : Sonali Publications. ISBN 81-8411-086-3.

Vijaya Bharathi, D., Author and Digumarti Bhaskara Rao, Editor (2000). *Educational Philosophies of Swami Vivekananda and John Dewey.* New Delhi : APH Publishing House. ISBN 81-7648-309-9.

Vijaya Bharathi, D., Author and Digumarti Bhaskara Rao, Editor (2005). *Educational Philosophy of John Dewey.* New Delhi : Discovery Publishing House. ISBN 81-8356-024-5.

Vijaya Bharathi, D., Author and Digumarti Bhaskara Rao, Editor (2005). *Educational Philosophy of Swami Vivekananda.* New Delhi : Discovery Publishing House. ISBN 81-8356-023-7.

Vijaya Lakshmi, D., Author and Digumarti Bhaskara Rao, Editor (2004) *Basic Education.* New Delhi : Discovery Publishing House. ISBN 81-7141-881-3.

Vijaya Lakshmi, V., Author and Digumarti Bhaskara Rao, Editor (2006). *Techniques of Teaching Music.* New Delhi : Sonali Publications. ISBN 81-8411-038-3.

Vijaya Kumar, S.J., Author and Digumarti Bhaskara Rao, Editor (2006). *Techniques of Teaching Mathematics.* New Delhi : Sonali Publications. ISBN 81-8411-039-1.

Visalakshi, V., Author and Digumarti Bhaskara Rao, Editor (2006). *Techniques of Teaching Biology.* New Delhi : Sonali Publications. ISBN 81-8411-045-6.

Visalakshi, V., Author and Digumarti Bhaskara Rao, Editor (2007). *Techniques of Teaching Zoology.* New Delhi : Sonali Publications. ISBN 81-8411-055-3.

**Books in Telugu Language**

Bhaskara Rao, Digumarti (1986). *Dhrushya Sravana Bodhanapakaranalu* (Audio Visual Teaching Aids). Guntur : Nagarjuna Publishers.

Bhaskara Rao, Digumarti (1993). *Jeevasashtra Bodhana* (Teaching of Biology). Guntur : Nagarjuna Publishers.

Bhaskara Rao, Digumarti (1995). *Vignanasasthra Bodhana* (Teaching of Science) Guntur : Nagarjuna Publishers.

Bhaskara Rao, Digumarti (1994). *Vidya Manovignana Sastram* (Educational Psychology). Guntur : Nagarjuna Publishers.

Bhaskara Rao, Digumarti (1997). *Vidya Manovignana Sastram* (Educational Psychology). Guntur : Creative Press.

Bhaskara Rao, Digumarti (1998). *DSC Study Material.* Guntur : Nagarjuna Publishers.

Bhaskara Rao, Digumarti (1998). *Upadhyayudu Vidya.* (Teacher and Education) Guntur : Nagarjuna Publishers.

Bhaskara Rao, Digumarti (1998). *Vidya Drukpadalu* (Perspectives of Education). Guntur : Nagarjuna Publishers.

Bhaskara Rao, Digumarti (1999). *EdCET Teaching Aptitude.* Guntur : Nagarjuna Publishers.

Bhaskara Rao, Digumarti (2001). *Bharata Samajamulo Upadyayudu Vidhya* (Teacher and Education in Emerging Indian Society). Guntur: Sri Nagarjuna Publishers.

Bhaskara Rao, Digumarti (2001). *Bhoutika Sastra Bodhana Padhatulu* (Methods of Teaching Physical Science). Guntur : Sri Nagarjuna Publishers.

Bhaskara Rao, Digumarti (2001). *Jeeva Sastra Bodhana Padhatulu* (Methods of Teaching Biology).Guntur : Sri Nagarjuna Publishers.

Bhaskara Rao, Digumarti (2001). *Vidya Manovignana Sastram* (Educational Psychology). Guntur : Sri Nagarjuna Publishers.

Bhaskara Rao, Digumarti (2003). *Patasala Yajamanyam / Paripalana* (School Management and Administration). Guntur : Sri Nagarjuna Publishers.

Bhaskara Rao, Digumarti and M. Srihari (2009). *Vardamana Bharata Desamulo Vidya* (Education in Emerging India). Guntur : Sri Nagarjuna Publishers.

Bhaskara Rao, Digumarti and B. Prasad Babu (2009). *Vidya Manovignana Sastram* (Educational Psychology). Guntur : Sri Nagarjuna Publishers.

Bhaskara Rao, Digumarti and B. Prasad Babu (2009). *Pradhamika Vidya mariyu Vileena Vidya Dhrukpadhalu* (Perspectives in Primary Education and Inclusive Education). Guntur : Sri Nagarjuna Publishers.

Bhaskara Rao, Digumarti and K. Subba Rao (2009). *Elementary Vidya, Pranalika, Yajamanyam, Upadyaya Kartavyalu* (Elementary Education, Planning, Management and Teacher Functions). Guntur: Sri Nagarjuna Publishers.

Bhaskara Rao, Digumarti and G. Prasanthi (2009). *Samardya Nirmanamu* (Capacity Building). Guntur : Sri Nagarjuna Publishers.

Bhaskara Rao, Digumarti and A. Jagadish (2009). *Vignansastra Bodhana Padhatulu* (Methods of Teaching Science).Guntur : Sri Nagarjuna Publishers.

Bhaskara Rao, Digumarti, Editor (2010). *Vardamana Bharata Desamulo Vidya – Question Bank* (Education in Emerging India). Guntur : Sri Nagarjuna Publishers.

Bhaskara Rao, Digumarti, Editor (2010). *Vidya Manovignana Sastram—Question Bank* (Educational Psychology). Guntur : Sri Nagarjuna Publishers.

Bhaskara Rao, Digumarti, Editor (2010). *Pradhamika Vidyamariyu Vileena Vidya Dhrukpadhalu—Question Bank* (Perspectives in Primary Education and Inclusive Education). Guntur : Sri Nagarjuna Publishers.

Bhaskara Rao, Digumarti, Editor (2010). *Elementary Vidya, Pranalika, Yajamanyam, Upadyaya Kartavyalu—Question Bank* (Elementary Education, Planning, Management and Teacher Functions). Guntur : Sri Nagarjuna Publishers.

Bhaskara Rao, Digumarti, Editor (2010). *Samardya Nirmanamu – Question Bank* (Capacity Building). Guntur : Sri Nagarjuna Publishers.

Bhaskara Rao, Digumarti, Editor (2010). *Ganithasastra Bodhana Padhatulu—Question Bank* (Methods of Teaching Science).Guntur: Sri Nagarjuna Publishers.

Bhaskara Rao, Digumarti, Editor (2010). *Vignansastra Bodhana Padhatulu—Question Bank* (Methods of Teaching Science).Guntur: Sri Nagarjuna Publishers.

Bhaskara Rao, Digumarti, Editor (2010). *Sanghikasastra Bodhana Padhatulu—Question Bank* (Methods of Teaching Social Studies).Guntur : Sri Nagarjuna Publishers.

Bhaskara Rao, Digumarti, Editor (2010). *Telugu Bodhana Padhatulu—Question Bank* (Methods of Teaching Social Studies).Guntur : Sri Nagarjuna Publishers.

Bhaskara Rao, Digumarti, Editor (2010). *Methods of Teaching English—Question Bank*. Guntur : Sri Nagarjuna Publishers.

Bhaskara Rao, Digumarti, N. Saraja, J. Lalitha and V. Mrunalini, Translators (2008). *Vidya—Samajam (Education—Society). Hyderabad* : Dr. B. R. Ambedkar Open University.

Gopala Krishna, G., A. Rama Krishna, K. Subba Rao and Bhaskara Rao, Digumarti (2004). *Jeevasashtra Bodhana Padhatulu* (Methods of Teaching of Biological science). Guntur : Sri Nagarjuna Publishers.

Krishna Murthy, V., K.S. Sudheer Reddy and Digumarti Bhaskara Rao (2004). *Vidya Manovignana Sastra Adharalu* (Foundations of Educational Psychology). Guntur : Sri Nagarjuna Publishers.

Lalini, V., V. Dayakara Reddy, M. Srihari and Digumarti Bhaskara Rao (2004). *Vidya Adharalu* (Foundations of Education). Guntur : Sri Nagarjuna Publishers.

Sastry, G.E.P. and G. Satya Narayana, Authors, Bhaskara Rao, Digumarti, Editor (2009). *Sanghikasastra Bodhana Padhatulu* (Methods of Teaching Social Studies).Guntur : Sri Nagarjuna Publishers.

Subba Rao, K.P., P. Ayodhya and Digumarti Bhaskara Rao (2004). *Patasala Yajamanyam—Vidhya Vyavasthalu* (School Management and Systems of Education). Guntur : Sri Nagarjuna Publishers.

Sudhakar, V., B. Ravindra Babu, D.S. Kumar and Digumarti Bhaskara Rao (2004). *Vidya Sanketika Sastram—Computer Vidhya* (Educational Technology and Computer Education). Guntur : Sri Nagarjuna Publishers.

# Index

## N



## O



## P



## R